I Never Came Home

I Never Came Home

Robert L. Scheck

READERSMAGNET, LLC

I Never Came Home
Copyright © 2017 by Robert L. Scheck

Published in the United States of America
ISBN Paperback: 978-1-947765-32-0
ISBN eBook: 978-1-947765-33-7

All rights reserved. No part of this publication may be reproduced, stored in a retrieval system or transmitted in any way by any means, electronic, mechanical, photocopy, recording or otherwise without the prior permission of the author except as provided by USA copyright law.

No lines, parts and quotations was taken from other books or any previous publications.

The opinions expressed by the author are not necessarily those of ReadersMagnet, LLC.

ReadersMagnet, LLC
80 Broad Street, 5th & 6th Floors Finance District | New York City, NY 10004 USA
1.646. 880. 9760 | www.readersmagnet.com

Book design copyright © 2017 by ReadersMagnet, LLC. All rights reserved.
Cover design by Ericka Walker
Interior design by Shieldon Watson

ACKNOWLEDGEMENTS

Thank you to all the following
Covenant Partners:

Vi & Richard Vigil
Commerce City, Colorado

Mel & Cathy Coleman
CMC Ministries Broomfield Colorado

Marvin Simoneau
Friend of God Ministry Now in heaven

Dr. Jeffrey H. & Jana F. Lowe
Lifetime Dental Care, Hays, KS

Rudolph L. Baca
Albuquerque, NM

Diana Kramer
Sower of Seeds Ministry, Kansas City, MO

Kirk & Treva Johnston
Shiloh Vineyards, Trego County, KS

Dr. Jeffrey & Katherine E. Burnett
Covenant Builders, Hays KS

DEDICATION

THIS WORK IS dedicated first to the Holy Spirit, who guided my footsteps through the mine fields of Viet Nam and still continues throughout my life; to Jesus Christ, the greatest soldier of all; and my heavenly Father, who knew me and called me before the foundations of the earth. Secondly, my wife who inspired me to write this book and was my editor. Finally, let this serve as a request for forgiveness to all those I've hurt while under war's influence and as an honorable salute to all those soldiers and families serving their country.

CONTENTS

★ ★ ★

Acknowledgements 5

Dedication 7

Foreword 13

Introduction 17

Chapter One
From "Happy Days"
On My Way To "Hell" 21

Chapter 2
Boot Camp—
Preparing For Hell 29

Chapter 3
Advanced Individual
Training (Ait), Bound For War 35

Chapter 4
"The Arrival" 41

Chapter 5
The Countdown—
365, 364, 363 45

Chapter 6
  Who's The Enemy? 49

Chapter 7
  The True Enemy
  Revealed 55

Chapter 8
  Chu Lai—
  My New Home—
  L Z Bayonet Not
  Club Med.................................. 59

Chapter 9
  A Night To Remember 63

Chapter 10
  Tenessee Goes Home 69

Chapter 11
  My First Ambush,
  Short Of Heroic 75

Chapter 12
  Death Rears Its
  Ugly Head 79

Chapter 13
  Drugs—One Means Of
  Temporary Escape 83

Chapter 14
  My First Good
  "Spiritual Encounter" 91

Chapter 15
  Many "Close Calls" 97

Chapter 16
  "Out Of Harm's Way" 105

Chapter 17
  My Epiphany 111

Chapter 18
  Letters Sent Home 117

Chapter 19
  Rest & Relaxation? 123

Chapter 20
  A Letter From My Brother 127

Chapter 21
  Now, Six More
  Months To Go 133

Chapter 22
  Part Time Friendships,
  Full Time Memories 137

Chapter 23
  The "Freedom Bird" 143

Chapter 24
  Back Home In The
  Good Old Usa 149

Chapter 25
  Majoring In Diversion,
  Minoring In Relationship 153

Chapter 26
  Where Is Love?........................161

Chapter 27
  Coming Home For
  The First Time........................165

Chapter 28
  My Final Thoughts
  To Those Coming
  Back Home From War...............169

FOREWORD

LIFE DURING THE era and escalation of the war in Viet Nam became very difficult and impacted our entire community. The traumatic events of that war and those that later followed left many with wounded hearts, especially those of the women left behind, the mothers, the wives, the sisters, the daughters, and friends of the soldiers that they loved and lost. I was one of those relationally involved with families.

I can't begin to describe or verbalize how I felt when first I heard that my high school classmates were going to Viet Nam. It tainted and ruined, what was up until then, a perfect adolescent existence. Now and forever I would be carrying the weight of their fate and destiny in my heart. I wish I could say my faith got me through those days but the truth is I was so emotionally affected that worry and my vivid imagination actually led me. The thoughts of them suffering, being miserable away from home or possibly not ever returning were always on my mind. I couldn't even watch the T.V. news. I feared I would perhaps see one of them.

Each time the bad news came over the phone at night that one of them had been killed both that night and the following week were extremely depressing and devastating for me. It literally shook my simple world. Even after graduation a fatality report always deeply disturbed me. The toughest ones, however, were when I was told my brother-in-law and cousin had been killed. I don't think you ever really get over the memory of those losses. Every time there was a family function there was a void because they were not there.

When I married Robert he would sometimes give an account of what you are about to read in this book. I could relate and communicate with him because I understood the pain of loss of my friends, brother-in-law and cousin. Each time I listened to him those feelings would come back. We spoke of them only occasionally due to the time that was necessary for healing.

Our son Angelo followed in his father Robert's footsteps and also joined the U. S. Army. He just recently finished his 14 month tour of Iraq. So once again that familiar emotional feeling, especially now dealing with your own son and his possible fate returned. However this time, as a mother, I don't think any of the roles I played before was as tense as this one.

In his book, *"I Never Came Home,"* Robert has offered his readers an educational tool to be used as a possible antidote and cure for both men and women experiencing directly or indirectly the emotional trauma associated with war. Through his personal transparency and writing style he has softened this serious subject matter with his humor and positive solutions for one's spirit, soul and body.

It is his real life story of how he has overcome his war experience, received his healing, and offers the reader an equation of how to do the same. Everyone has a war they are going through in their own heart. I pray this book will help bring closure to like situations. It has already helped many. It really has helped me. We hope in some way it will heal your heart.

Jill Vigil Scheck

INTRODUCTION

REVISIT WITH ME, a 1946 Baby Boomer from Denver, Colorado, an extraordinary episode in my life's journey during and after the Viet Nam War. When your loved ones return from the recent war in Iraq what will you expect? To this very day, we have yet to learn how to care for those suffering from the trauma of the 9/11 terrorist attack, the most recent hurricanes, flood disasters, such as Katrina, tsunamis or the increasing damage of hurricanes and tornadoes. How have you dealt thus far with the mass killings in our schools? What does a person expect to find when he first arrives home, if indeed, there is still a home that remains? How long will it take for everyone to adjust? Is anyone really prepared to deal with the aftereffects of war, natural disasters or even today's divorce epidemic and handle with sensitivity each layer of damage to all those affected? Have you ever heard the statement, "War isn't over when it's over? Better yet, have you ever experienced and felt any of the above realities? Those who have been involved in any form of war and the like to any degree, whether directly or indirectly as a family member or friend can attest to the lingering emotional aftermath. War, disasters and divorce destroy people, relationships, property, land and all living things caught in their wake. They contaminate the environment with things we sometimes cannot see but nonetheless feel. They can grab an ordinarily cheerful person, change his former identity, alter the course of his future and sometimes return him so dark, as if he were a total stranger. The flashbacks, the overall depth of woundedness, the intensity of personal loss and the obstinacy of one's memory will prove to be all too recurrent. Is there some way to finally release their emotional, physical and spiritual consequences? Can the results of all wars, whether those between nations, between gangs, between family members, between man and nature and even those in process in the thoughts and intents of the heart of man ever be eradicated? Are we on an unstoppable collision course with total destruction?

"War specifically! What is it good for? Absolutely nothing! I'll say it again…" Remember those song words, a familiar lyric and the sentiment of the majority from the Viet Nam era? The very nature of war by dictionary definition is a conflict, battle, or contest carried on by force of arms. By design man was not originally created for conflict, battles or force. Force comes by control or might. How do you feel when someone is controlling or forcing you by might to do anything?

How helpless does the destruction of a tornado or a hurricane with winds in excess of 145 miles per hour leave you? They are an attack against our very nature which was designed to have dominion and never to be dominated, yet they have their very origin from our own fallen condition. Herein lies the paradox. However, somewhere hidden in this seeming contradiction is the solution to our fragile human predicament. The "good news" is that there has been provided for us a means of departure, a healthy disconnection and a total healing from the ravages of war and its relatives.

This book recounts a journey through one of these cataclysms from a Christian soldier relating his first hand experience of war. It deals with three realms of warfare that are experienced and equally shared with any traumatic event: (1) the physical external realm; (2) the internal thought/emotional realm; and finally (3) the spiritual realm. The twofold purpose for writing this book is: (1) to offer the reader a historical text of what a typical individual soldier faces before, during and after war times, and (2) to offer those affected by war or the like both a hope and a means of escape from the chains of emotional captivity rooted all the way down to one's deepest heart level. For those who choose to relate to the author's experiences that follow specifically regarding his time in the Viet Nam War, those he encountered, conquered and brought to conclusion, this narrative can possibly extend emancipation from the victimization and devastation caused by like past experiences.

This work presents optimism with understanding, not only to war veterans and their families, but also to all those who have returned recently and those who are entangled right now in the current war in Iraq and elsewhere internationally in the now, ever present war with "Terrorism" and including our current disasters. It is the author's desire that, by sharing his experiences and the wisdom he gained that followed regarding this subject, the reader will be empowered to reconcile and restore his life and his family to once again walk in wholeness, joy and peace.

I dedicate this book first to the Holy Spirit, who has guided my steps through the minefields of life and Viet Nam. Secondly, I devote this work to my wife, family and to all those men, women and families, who served and experienced first hand all the emotional heartache associated with war's havoc and similar tribulation.

Let this serve as an explanation of what most soldiers were experiencing with an understanding and possibly a help for emotional closure regarding those who ultimately had to lay down their lives without leaving behind a written account. *

CHAPTER 1

FROM "HAPPY DAYS" ON MY WAY TO "HELL"

HAVE YOU EVER awakened in the morning and your first thought upon rousing was "Where am I?" Perhaps the last dream you were involved in was so vivid that you thought you were there. But when you realized it was only a dream and at that just a bad dream, you were so relieved you were actually at home in your bed and that dream place was just a replay of the past. Where does that rerun come from? Where is it stored? Why do those past events continue to repeat? The answer to this is they have been stored in the memory of your heart. Were you aware that all matter has memory? I'm not only referring to your physical, material heart but also to your spiritual heart that I will later explain. Science has found that the heart has more long-term memory cells than the brain. Your heart's memory capacity is strongly influenced by the intensity of the emotions that accompanied past events. So, now I will begin to relate some of the events that have affected my heart's memory and take the reader back to my journey relating to war, specifically the War in Viet Nam.

My life's journey began by winning the lottery. No kidding, it really happened! One day, somewhere in Tacoma Washington, approximately nine months before August 31, 1946, I entered a marathon race with over two million participants. My father, who met my mother shortly after World War 2, and in the spirit of post war celebration and joy, decided to enroll me in the event. I won! I came in first with of course mom playing a major role in the victory. Without her accommodating choice to also participate, the triumph would have been impossible. I won! I made it! One of my greatest highs on planet earth was first winning this lottery. It was for me D-day, the day I was conceived by my wonderful parents and thus the beginning of my life. The seed had been planted and now its harvest appeared. Wow! I'm here! I've been given a chance to live and make a "run for it," and go for the gold. I was born with a positive attitude. Why? I'll have to tell you the details about that later.

Have any of you had recollection of your early years as an infant? The first remembrance of my existence was when I was somewhere around four years old. I can't remember my participation in all the stories my mother told and retold me about the years before then. She said our first house was a remodeled chicken coup. That possibly explains why I was hesitant to learn how to crawl and walk. Have you heard about the young boy who dropped his gum in the chicken yard and thought he found it three times before he did? She assured me, however, that the floor had been cleaned thoroughly.

At two years of age I took my first airplane ride from Tacoma to Denver, Colorado, which would be my new home. I probably slept most of the way, which I still do every time I travel by plane. I was also told we lived in the "Lincoln Park Projects," a name given to the low-income housing for the military. Like I said, I remember nothing. But, as far as I was concerned, I believe it was great. In the 1948—52 backdrop of middle-class America USA, mine was a common environment. So, let the good times roll.

4992 Grove Street was the first address I remembered and the first house we owned and called home. There's just something about one's "home." GE-3-2382 was my first telephone number. I wasn't sure why I could remember those things. My awareness of early childhood was a bit fuzzy, like being a friendly little potato put into a corner to observe the world and then coming to life all of a sudden at four. My first remembrance and celebration that I was alive came at my cognizance of riding my tricycle, loving it and enjoying my neighborhood's scenery. My house (all 650 square feet of it) seemed so huge, and my tricycle so tall.

Yes, I know, it was because I was so small. Back then chocolate chip cookies were larger, Peter Pan peanut butter and jelly sandwiches were my favorite and they were much bigger and tasted better. Kool-Aid washed it all down with a sugar blast. What a delightful perspective of size, people, and food a child has. I can remember the physical closeness and the embrace of mom. Loved life! My heart thought, "so far, so good." Why I was here on planet earth was not my concern at the time. But I had a strong perception that I was, that I existed.

Being born in 1946 and raised in the 50's, just another typical "baby boomer" in the great environmental backdrop of Denver, Colorado was idyllic. Back then, Denver was simple, had clean air, little traffic, plenty of recreational areas for kids and the children in the neighborhood had down-to-earth fun and were uncomplicated characters right out of "Leave it to Beaver." I was Wally and my brother, the "Beave." We knew all the kids and families on our block on 50th & Grove Street and one out of every five of our friends looked like Opie Taylor of Mayberry, RFD and were just as simple. Grade school was within walking distance and the beautiful summers seemed to last forever. For my grandchildren's sake they should know that their grandfather walked about seven blocks on the way to school and five to ten miles on the way back home each day. Would you believe one?

High school truly was much like the movies "Grease" and "American Graffiti" combined. What a gas! My adolescent life resembled the TV series "Happy Days" for the most part. Sports, letter sweaters, girlfriends, going steady, pizza parlors, dances, music unparalleled, fun, fun, and more fun were the day's ingredients. The sequence of life's ladder of progression at that time was birth, childhood, elementary school, high school, college for some, and ultimately for the majority marriage, kids, job, old age, death, heaven and thus the cycle completed. You simply went from one to the next, much like a robot, without thinking outside that box.

Then in 1963, as I sat in the classroom of a typical school day, our world was shaken with the announcement over the school's p.a. system, "President Kennedy has been assassinated! A reality cloud of emotion filled with tears formed as it came over everyone and penetrated the very depth of one's being. This was to be soon followed in history by the deathly thunderstorm called, "The War in Viet Nam." The happy bubble of "life in Disneyland" had burst. Music itself had been altered, the very atmosphere was contaminated with fear and confusion as the military "draft" was dragging high school and college students out from their comfortable desks and homes into either the battlefields of Southeast Asia or into the battle zones of rebellion of life in the "hood."

What had happened? This environmental Atomic Bomb had exploded and its destruction and devastating aftermath couldn't be totally measured.

It affected the heart, philosophy, spirituality, morality and integrity of the nation, state, city, community, society, church, families, marriages, and the children. War! Humanity's definitive failure! It's not going to be over even when its agenda was scheduled to be over.

I entered Regis College in 1965 with the backdrop of the selective military draft and the war in Viet Nam ever calling. College students tried to avoid the draft by applying the 2 S (full-time college student) draft deferment. We were hoping that by the end of our four-year school term the war would be over. Studies, exams, sports, friends, parties, women, and much beer, offered temporary escape in an attempt to pleasantly pass the time but the ever-present reality of war continued pressing upon my ever-reminding awareness.

It was soon to be inevitable. A couple of months after graduating in 1969 I received a letter from my uncle, his name, Sam. He sent his "Greetings" with an invitation for a two-year expense paid scholarship, which included room and board and an opportunity to travel to the Orient. It would require that I relinquish all the job opportunities that I had lined up according to my four years of education and college degree in favor of this excellent offer. It was, however, more like an offer from the "Godfather," one I shouldn't refuse. Besides the alternative option included state issue attire and no travel for four years and I never did look good in stripes. There was a special added attraction to this opportune occasion, leaving my wife and daughter at home alone while all the male bonding took their place. This was going to be such a great deal, so well advertised and marketed, that only a fool would pass it up.

Sarcasm, Stop! Please excuse me. This is how I was feeling. All kidding aside, this is the sacrifice one must make to leave his "home" and serve the country he loves when his country goes to war. The cost for all involved will be suffering, many will be wounded outwardly, all will be affected inwardly, and the price for some will be their very life.

"I'm O.K. so far, I thought, after all, something might occur to change the reality of my dilemma before I have to actually go downtown and report for duty." Maybe I wouldn't pass the physical! Get serious! If you could fog a mirror, you could pass the physical. Besides, I was as healthy as a horse after spending four years in collegiate sports. The results of the physical—Pass! All of this being said, my life experiences and the sum total memory of them, is who I have become. It is my present reality and IDENTITY.*

CHAPTER 2

BOOT CAMP—PREPARING FOR HELL

RELUCTANTLY I WOKE up that day to the cry of my obnoxious alarm clock and wished it were all just a bad dream. As I left the comfort of home, I kissed my family goodbye as I was dropped off to walk into that cold government building where about fifty young men were about to leave Denver headed for Fort Campbell, Kentucky. I went through the motions of being obedient as a programmed robot and responsible citizen each time they called out my last name, not really knowing what to expect or what I was about to experience in my first taste of life in the military. There is definitely a major difference in attitude between a draftee and one who enlists of their own volition. My attitude clearly sucked!

The airplane ride was short, the bus ride to the base even shorter. We were immediately greeted at the bus door upon exiting by some screaming, rather unfriendly and rude people called drill sergeants, who were nothing like the amiable recruiting sergeants back home. "Get off my bus you miserable "*/&5*@%" trainees and double time, ho!" were their first words of greeting and hospitality. The pressure and stress started that day and never really ended. I knew from this point on when the senior drill sergeant said to all of us, "Boys, (not men) today your soul might belong to God but your ass belongs to me," that this was not going to be a real pleasant spa vacation at Club Med.

As I left my home, my neighborhood, my family, my friends, my custom Chevy, my clothes and all my neat stuff behind, I met a new friend, who became real familiar, called abandonment. Now also, on the very first day, I left all my hair, (my well-trained Hollywood style—"Do", that took years to groom) on the barber's floor. I do thank them however for the green ball cap that covered my now bald head. If it weren't for my 2 ears stopping that green cap, I would have been blind. They took my nice tailored civilian clothes and swapped me for some ungodly olive drab apparel, not ever to be in fashion and three sizes too large in exchange. The footwear I was given I could never wear to the prom. They were ugly, heavy black boots unsuitable for running or recreation. Oh, I get it now. Boot camp! Now I made the connection, my ass and his boot. That pretty much summed up our relationship with the drill sergeants. They all went to the school of "mean" and graduated with a degree in "nasty." The first week we were told there was no room for us there in Kentucky, so they immediately bused us to Fort Benning, Georgia. "Maybe the drill sergeants there would be a little more understanding," so I thought. After all, (and I have never been prejudiced) I continued thinking because all of them were black and I was "honkie" white, perhaps there was someone at the next stop who would love me with some compassion. Not in this case, they all were honor students and alumni of Mean & Nasty University graduating "summa cum nasty!" They treated men of any color equally, boorishly.

I was stripped of everything I held dear including my former dignity and athletic fame and self-esteemed popularity. So, now I'm wearing dog tags around my neck with my name and serial number for identification. Dog tags! Does that tell you anything? Very impersonal, wouldn't you say? It does give you a hint of what one with dog tags will soon be eating! This was only a preview of bad on its way to worse.

The boot camp's agenda was the following: training, discipline, humility and/or humiliation. Did I forget to mention one of the daily activities was picking up cigarette butts? I hated that so much. I wasn't even a smoker. That just was not fair. It was so much beneath my dignity and station in life to pick up after someone else's bad habit. As if I didn't have enough nonsense to deal with—foreign butts! It was difficult.

Drill sergeants made my high school football coach look like a choirboy. I weighed about 230 pounds when I showed up to boot camp and was in good shape but the sergeant said, "you're too big, we only weigh 180 pounds in this man's army!" With that fine compliment, he kept his eye on me for a while to see if I could physically perform all the rigors of military life. Again, I passed. Actually, I was in the best shape of my life at 260 pounds by the end of basic training and still had a 32-inch waist. I resembled a veritable GI Joe on the outside but was a displaced, wretched human being on the inside. With my bald head my friends called me Mr. Clean.

When boot camp finally ended after eight miserable weeks, we were somewhat relieved. During the classroom training courses I tried to outsmart the tests for my new military occupation. The last thing I wanted to be permanently was an infantryman, a "grunt" as they called it, a ground-pounder. After all, I was a somewhat sophisticated college graduate, so, surely they would give me a desk job or something comparable. So, for example, on some of the written tests, they asked questions like, "Do you like the out of doors?" I answered, "No." "Do you like camping out and fishing?" I answered, "No." "Do you like shooting guns?" I answered, "No." Certainly I have outsmarted these obvious psychological questions geared for those selected and headed for the infantry. We knew if we were to be infantry we would certainly be headed for Viet Nam. My test results came back for my <u>military occupational specialty</u> called MOS—INFANTRY! I later figured it out. It didn't make a difference what you scored, 0 to 100. Again, if you could even maybe fog a mirror, you're destined to be an infantryman.

Great, what's going to be my next surprise? You probably have guessed the surprise. For those with an infantry MOS they were rewarded with eight more weeks of infantry training much worse than boot camp. That simply meant more physical and mental discipline and of course picking up even more cigarette butts. Sixteen weeks of butt picking! I knew it was for personal discipline and dying to my pride, but, nevertheless, I was still incensed!*

CHAPTER 3

ADVANCED INDIVIDUAL TRAINING (AIT), BOUND FOR WAR

HAVE YOU EVER felt a real strong sense of destiny knocking? It happens to me all the time. It's somewhat like déjà vu but more like replaying one scene of the video of your life. I knew I was destined to go to Viet Nam yet I was trying to take any escape route to deter its inevitability. What made it worse was my ever-pressing imagination that told me, if I go there, I was going there to die. We all live with a certain degree of fear. Fear is a tormenting spirit. Fear's competitor is Faith or should I say, faith's adversary is fear. My faith was at that time in my life dormant at best. Instead of allowing faith to master my unavoidable destiny it defaulted to fear. Instead of my faith leading me, I was being ruled emotionally by fear. The nature of fear is that, if it is not stopped or replaced, it will continue to escalate until its intensity debilitates you and finally paralyzes you. That's what happened to me. That's what war, fighting, arguing and the like release, fear. It's a negative emotion heated by passion that removes one from any semblance of peace. The abandonment I was again feeling was rooted in fear. Now that I had begun to walk in fear I entered into an altered state of reality. Now I was walking in an illusionary world, one that I thought was true, and its final destination and climax was death in Viet Nam.

By now these men and this environment were what my life had to adapt to. My family and home became farther and farther distant. I was going to have to spend two years away from what was familiar for the last twenty one years and adjust to a whole new world called "life in the military." Some grown men wept at times because of missing their families and sometimes just from the frustration of the rigors of military discipline and verbal abuse. A few simply couldn't emotionally or physically handle it and were discharged for various weaknesses. One even attempted suicide and failed. To compound the tense atmosphere there were many racial confrontations in that era. There were people from all parts of the country with different cultural backgrounds but soon we all shared a common denominator, that is, we were all Americans and had to get through these tough times.

At Fort Polk, Louisiana, they trained us further in the use of the weaponry we were going to employ in war. We were now called "killing machines." This is not a label I cherished. I would have rather been labeled a "survivor." The only Army bases I knew were hot, followed by hotter, in preparation for "damn" hot. The P.T. (physical training) tests were weekly. I did so many push-ups you would think I was Jack La Lane. Hand-to-hand combat was taught. Using a bayonet at close range was taught. Are you kidding me? A couple of weeks of hand-to-hand combat and a couple of weeks of bayonet practice were just enough to tell me, if I had to use either, I was going to die slow and painfully. Let's get real. If you don't have extensive training in anything these days you are not going to be proficient. The only chance we had, if we had to fight at close range, is if the enemy was just as inefficient as we were. What would you think if a football team full of young men, who were only introduced to the game for a few months, had to play one game for 365 days, 24 hours a day and their lives were at stake depending on their knowledge of the sport? Anyway, this would be the team we send overseas every time there is a war that requires a draft. Many die in their rookie season. Granted, there were professionals along with the rookies but they were few and far between and were vulnerable because of the weakest players.

Most of the discipline that came with training was disguised and camouflaged. One morning we were rudely awakened at 3 o'clock to stand at attention in the rain while the C.O. (Commanding Officer) was promoting his Saint Bernard puppy from Specialist 3 to Warrant Officer 2! That kind of nonsense always infuriated me. There was a funny guy named Miller from New York, who was in the National Reserve, going through the training with us. He was a kick in the pants. He joked about everything. He did K.P. (kitchen police) and peeled potatoes almost every day as punishment for his attitude. The C.O. told Miller, "if you didn't dig a hole with your entrenching tool big enough to bury a "deuce and a half" truck by the end of this final week of training, your orders were going to be changed to Viet Nam." We would daily walk by that hole, (Miller's underground garage) that he was digging, to see a very small shovel full of dirt leaving the pit with Miller still inside. The final day arrived and the C.O. came out to inspect the hole. He drove the truck into the pit, drove it out, got out of the imposing truck, flicked his cigarette butt into the enormous hole and said to Miller, "you have one day to bury this butt." To our amazement, he managed to fill it up that day with a "little help" from his friends. So, Miller went back to New York instead of Viet Nam. The captain later told us it was all a lie about changing his orders. Things like that were ways of breaking us down for eventual obedience to orders. Do you think it could have been the C.O. that was responsible for **all** the butts I had to pick up?

Finally AIT came to an end. That final day all two hundred of us in "C" Company stood at attention in rank to receive our orders for our next assignment. The first name was read—destination Germany, the second name—also Germany. Immediately I thought, "maybe I'll also be going to Germany." However, the next 198 names that proceeded to be read one at a time loudly declared, "destination, Republic of Viet Nam." They could have just said that the rest of us were going to Viet Nam but instead they repeated it one hundred and ninety eight times until I can still hear that sound today—Republic of Viet Nam.*

CHAPTER 4

"THE ARRIVAL"

After leaving Fort Polk with my eminent orders to Viet Nam, I wanted to somehow avoid and escape that reality and leave planet earth. "Beam me up, Scottie, please!" Often I had a recurring dream throughout my childhood that now and then would torment me when I was already out of sorts. I would dream that I was in the front yard of my house playing when my dad, mom, brother and sisters proceeded to get into the car and leave. I would say, "Don't leave me here alone. I want to go with you." They said as they waived goodbye, "We're just going to the store, don't worry, we'll be right back." The very moment they went around the corner and were out of sight, a group of three, mean boys, with evil intentions came around that same corner to beat me up. They would beat on me until I woke myself up. The dream happened so regularly and felt so real that as soon as I saw them approaching I would stick my fingers into my eye sockets while still asleep to force my eyes to open in order to end another identical episode. The key words here are: <u>don't leave me alone</u> and <u>don't worry</u>. That familiar feeling of abandonment, my old friend, was back again and his two friends, "Worry and Anxiety" that always accompanied him, were what I was now feeling on my way home on my first military leave.

The brief time of military leave at home with my family soon passed. The thought of my certain death continued to haunt me. It came to the point where I selfishly and in desperation wanted to have another child during this short home visit, hoping to at least leave another namesake behind. Of course, that was a totally selfish act on my part. I didn't see it then because "selfish" was my middle name. My motives were solely emotional led and regretfully dishonorable, driven by fear. Nevertheless, the "mother to be" would oblige and successfully became pregnant at that time. This certainly doesn't invalidate the worth of that precious child. I overstayed my leave, played hooky for a while and was AWOL (Away Without Leave) for a couple of weeks. Scared that at any moment a knock at the door would come, I chose to report, though late, for duty at the Denver Army Headquarters. This time, however, that I said goodbye prior to my flight to Viet Nam, little did I know that the person who just said goodbye to all would never come home again!

They sent me to California to then fly to Viet Nam with a whole new company of soldiers because my original company had left weeks earlier. My next destiny and assignment: The Americal Division, Charlie Company, 5/46 198th Chu Lai, Viet Nam.

During the flight on the 747 stretch jet, suited to carry more than two hundred soldiers, I fantasized, like the optimist, who jumped off the Empire State Building and on his way down, around the fiftieth floor, and said, "Well, so far, so good!" The trip was to last about twenty-eight hours stopping only once in Japan for refueling. The hours slowly ticked by. It was getting closer and closer now as the captain of the plane continued to give us each latest air location. When he announced, "we were now entering the country of Viet Nam," there was a deathly silence that filled the plane's atmosphere. Then there came a shallow sound like an almost silent gasp of air from the invisible, sudden stopping of everyone's heartbeat. Reality was hitting like a hunter's arrow striking its prey.

My memory of the "Arrival" is all too vivid still today. As the plane started its descent, it was if we were descending into hell. We were all looking out the windows seeing helicopters in the sky below as they opened fire with machine guns into the hillsides. There were white smoke clouds from explosions cluttering the landscape everywhere I could see. It looked like miniature jeeps, military vehicles and people, the size of ants all hurrying in a state of panic. I saw fire in the trees beneath and could hear the barrage of mortar fire below and felt the concussion. My first thoughts were, "Please don't land in all of this! This couldn't be what it is going to be like for an entire year! Are we even going to be able to land without getting blown up in the air?" We landed safely amid all of the chaos and confusion and hustled off the airplane to cover.

Upon landing in Ben Hoa, for my first breath of air I was only able to in-hell, I mean inhale. I couldn't breath. It was so hot, muggy, totally sand desert with such high humidity and it wasn't any air I had ever been exposed to breathe in. Fear of not being able to breath hit me with the weight of an asthmatic attack. Everyone was gasping for air as his lungs were frantically trying to acclimate to this foreign climate to survive from suffocation, much like that of the exposure to poisonous gas fumes. At last I could take in a breath. Finally I could exhale and inhale in rhythm voluntarily once again. This unfriendly welcome was just the beginning and only a preview of my war tour in hell that was about to escalate from terrible to dreadful. Would I be going to die here in hell or have I already?*

CHAPTER 5

THE COUNTDOWN—365, 364, 363...

THERE WAS A story of an old man in his nineties who lived meagerly in a basement rental apartment. Above on the main floor there lived a young man in his early twenties who also rented during his four years of college. There was quite a contrast of life styles as you can imagine both dealing with life issues at the same time while sharing the same dwelling. The young man would occasionally have beer parties on the weekends, playing loud music into the early morning, not paying any attention to the noise he was making atop the sleeping quarters of the old man. The elderly man would seldom leave his room because his health was ever so slowly dwindling. At times he would go to the corner store for groceries if his monthly check came in the mail.

One day the little man took his last breath and passed away after a long battle with sickness. No one even knew he was dying and what made it worse was no one even checked to see if he was still alive that day. Two weeks passed by as the college man continued to party as usual and live it up while only a twelve-inch thick floor separated the evidence of death below.

The tragedy and moral of the story is that often times we simply are not aware of how the other half of our world is struggling for their very existence while we are eating, drinking and making merry.

When the TV news would come on during my college days I remember watching the footage of live fighting in Viet Nam. The soldiers would jump out of the helicopters into rice paddies with gunshots everywhere and run to cover in the rain and mud. I thought, "Man, I'm glad that's not me." I knew it was really happening but because I wasn't feeling it first hand, it had very little effect on me. Besides, I thought, "that is way over there." It was kind of like seeing a hitchhiker on the road on a cold day, thinking about it, but not stopping to pick him up. I would just turn the channel to the football game and forget about the news and all that reality T.V.

Now, I'm that guy way over there ten thousand miles from the comforts of home jumping out of a hovering helicopter into black, wet and stinky, rice paddy mud with bullets flying everywhere. Now it's my turn in the basement of the world with no one on the main floor USA caring about me fighting for my life while they continued to party. Now I'm the one they are looking at on the TV news! Watching it and living it are two different realms of reality. It is one thing to watch John Wayne get shot and killed in one war movie and come back the next movie and still be alive and well. It's another thing when you are up against real bullets and shedding real blood that can determine if you just might have the lead role in your final performance. Hollywood is fiction as are its events. Meanwhile, the actors arrive at the sneak previews in tuxedoes. War is fact and lethal as are its events while many of its heroes go home in body bags. For some it will be their final curtain call.

The first night, day 365, after adapting to the air in Ben Hoa, we were being prepared to go to Chu Lai. That night there were no confrontations. Well, maybe there was one. There was a very small outside drive-in movie screen and about fifty or so benches for the troops to watch a film. About ten minutes into the movie I noticed all those in the front row getting up and running towards the rear area, they were followed by those in the next row and then the next row, and then I heard someone yell, "Flying Cockroaches!" There was a dark moving cloud of huge insects swarming the entire area and chasing everything in their path in harm's way. There was never a dull moment here, always something strange and eerie. Even the insects, as I will tell you later, were small armies of enemies we were to face during our tour. These are the biggest flying cockroaches I have ever seen. Their bodies were the size of my index finger, big enough to wear a saddle and were everywhere we went. They made the "cucarachas" of Mexico look anemic.

A tradition of the soldier was to carry a small calendar with him to mark off each day until finally he was down to one. D-day! So far my first day was long and miserable but not as bad as those about to follow. I went to sleep that night hoping that this was only a bad dream but knowing not even forcing my eyelids open this night would help. My first priority was getting out of here alive and I wasn't sure what that would call for. Ever been in a contest and you didn't know who you were fighting or have a clue how to win? What if it was going to cost you your life and there was nothing to win? These thoughts continued accumulating in my heart's memory video bank.*

CHAPTER 6

WHO'S THE ENEMY?

EVERY DAY FROM within I questioned: "What is all of this really about, why am I here, what will I encounter today, will I live, will I be wounded and what will be my final destiny?" My heart's questions were never settled as to my overall purpose here, what I was fighting for or whom I was fighting and was all of this worth dying for? There were many unanswered queries with no apparent logical answers rolling around in my consciousness. These daily unanswered questions turned to worry, became negative emotions that increased my level of stress and internalized a masked pain. However at this point it now became evident to me there existed more than just one dimension and battlefield upon which I was fighting.

First of all, there was a constant struggle raging on the INSIDE of me in the realm of my thought life. What I was now experiencing diametrically contradicted my heart's belief system. One's thought life during wartime never seems to soften but instead drifts into a series of vain imaginations that usually end in a negative funk. I was taught to love not hate, to give life, not take it. My thoughts and my emotions were continually out of peace on that battlefield. This went on twenty four hours a day. I couldn't find the turn-off switch. Because my emotions were already influenced by fear, I was always just pretending and appearing to be O.K. while set on an automatic survival mode. The thinking torment never seemed to stop, only fade at times. By design human beings were not programmed to handle fear or stress but instead only trained to try to manage it. No one however was trained to handle the stress of war except through first hand experiencing its trials and errors.

The second battlefield on the OUTSIDE featured "Charlie" the generic name given to any Vietnamese person opposed to the U.S.A. being in his backyard and willing to kill anyone caught trespassing. Charlie was labeled the villain and was so designated the personal enemy to all of us. It was an imperfect prejudiced label but because everything that war perverted or contaminated in its association even that name now released a negative emotion when spoken. Charlie could be labeled a "Viet Cong", a seemingly good-guy citizen by day dressed in white, but a killer dressed in black pajamas at night. Charlie could be a "Zapper" or "Sapper," a Viet Cong trained to slither quietly, scantily clad through the dense rolled barbed wire fence bordering our bunkered complex to infiltrate our perimeter or turn our wired claymore mines backwards so that when we triggered them we would blow ourselves up. Charlie could be a "tunnel rat" hidden anywhere in an underground camouflaged maze of tunnels waiting for an opportunity to kill. Charlie might be a soldier in uniform of the North Vietnamese Army (N.V.A.), the title of the enemy's full scale trained army. We were trained to hate Charlie. We were given the overall directive to "Police" the country! The overwhelming, obvious, policing problem here was that most chose to hate the people we were trained to police and couldn't even tell who was who! In a shopping mall can you tell me who is from the south and who is from the north? The directive was to confront, capture, jail or if necessary kill all those from the north. It's not even a simple matter of geography. The difference between the north and the south could only be detected by a hidden attitude within.

In addition to these players and on that same battlefield of this real life drama, were the weapons infantrymen could encounter daily. Some of the war props you could see but most often could not see. Here's a list of a few:

- Land mines. The most famous called "Bouncing Bettys" which when depressed by the touch of a foot would bounce up to explode about waist high and usually destroy both legs or worse;

- "Pungi-Pits." Pits which were camouflaged and contained upright, sharpened, bamboo sticks treated on the tips with human feces so that when one a soldier fell in it would pierce and infect that body part;

- Entire North Vietnamese Army or as it is called NVA, complete with armored personnel carriers (tanks). (This is not to be confused with the GI Joe children's games and products. These are real and designed to be hazardous to your health.)

- 50—caliber machine guns set up in hidden bunkers;

- AK-47's—Russian-made semi-automatic rifles;

- Snipers hidden everywhere;

- People, even small children with bombs tied to their bodies hidden under clothing;

- An assortment of man-made devices, bombs, grenades and explosives meant to injure in any way;

- Mortars and rockets designed to cause extensive damage.

The irony of all this found on the second exterior battlefield level was Charlie and his toys were not even our primary enemy. The most common error a soldier makes in assessing the overall war picture is to conclude his most threatening adversary is a person. Charlie was just a pawn, a human puppet influenced, controlled and manipulated by an unknown evil force that was never seen, whose identity was an enigma, a riddle many still today have not deciphered. This evil force remains in an invisible realm headquartered in the third battlefield.*

CHAPTER 7

THE TRUE ENEMY REVEALED

IN ORDER TO understand any war and in order to exercise the wisdom necessary to defeat the real enemy, one must look deeper into its source and the realm from which it originated. War for the most part has been so misunderstood, so misrepresented, so underestimated and has been an endless merry-go-round of idle philosophies, opinions, debates, talk shows, books, movies, always falling short of its very definitive nature like a dog chasing his own tail in ignorance of its real derivation. I'm going to take a chance at possibly losing and irritating some of you readers by presenting the originating source and root system of all wars with the following revelation. Unless you are a student of war history, an educated military officer or one trained in spiritual warfare, this following premise is usually the last given consideration.

Allow me to identify that source and battlefield with a biblical reference. Starting in Ephesians Chapter 6 verse 10:

> *Finally, my brethren, be strong in the Lord and in the power of His might.* 11. *Put on the whole armor of God that you may be able to stand against the wiles of the devil.* 12. *For we do not wrestle against flesh and blood (people), but against principalities, against powers, against rulers of the darkness of this age, against spiritual hosts of wickedness in the heavenly places*

According to this scripture passage the origin and source of war itself emerges from the kingdom of darkness ruled by the devil and his armies called principalities, powers, rulers, and spiritual hosts of wickedness whose headquarters is located in heavenly places. It specifically points out our struggle should not be with people! Does this mean we were missing the real target?

Did I even have a clue back then regarding this principle? No way! I wasn't aware of anyone who fully understood that total concept of war. Now that doesn't imply that no one knew. This simply explains why most of us always felt we weren't winning. That's why no one can win without considering the impact and picture of the entire spiritual and natural panorama. I had literally come to a dead end in my limited understanding. This hidden factor had remained a mystery for most of us, that is, except for those leaders throughout history, who were led by the Spirit of God for wisdom. It will continue for those who never have been exposed to this realm of reality or refuse to accept it right now after hearing it. You don't have to believe the Word of God. You can choose to believe in something else. You don't have to believe in the principle of gravity for it to work. You can choose not to deal with either, however, if they are a reality, they will deal with you! Whichever you choose it will be your heart that is affected and programmed as it records the consequences of your choice.

Regarding this third battlefield, we were told we were fighting against something called Communism. I couldn't see this—ism, he had no face, he was responsible for promoting fear, but when I shot at the other human beings, I never felt the—ism could be killed. I could sense its presence. The backdrop of communism saturated the atmosphere and filled the air with an eerie darkness. Flesh and blood were being sacrificed in the physical realm. Somehow I knew that unless we killed every single one of the enemy who believed in this spirit of communism, its seed would perpetuate. I had the sense that I was fighting a spiritual entity and my mind now entered into its battlefield. Collectively, we never felt the sense of winning. The simple fact was that the confusion and chaos of the war we were fighting came from the unseen and unknown sources and the plain truth was we were not trained or equipped physically, emotionally nor spiritually with the means to obliterate a belief system.

Any spiritual war, whether against communism, or against today's terrorism, or even as the enemy has labeled us "capitalists" promoting capital-ism, has to somehow expire spiritually. However the paradox is that spirits don't die but must be put under authority. Body counts or body bags are not an indicator of winning war but instead all parties losing to ignorance. Even the death of a black widow spider will only come when all of its eggs are subjected to fire. Killing human beings, who were made in the image and likeness of God, for the cause of peace is another oxymoron that is actually the spirit of stupid going to seed due to the fact our real enemy is spiritual and invisible.*

CHAPTER 8

CHU LAI—MY NEW HOME—L Z BAYONET NOT CLUB MED

CHARLIE COMPANY 5/46TH 198th, Americal Division's home at the time I arrived from Ben Hoa was a bunkered military complex called "L Z Bayonet" located in Chu Lai, Viet Nam. This was to be my new neighborhood. Chu Lai had been in the headlines recently and was known for the infamous controversial event called the "Mai Lai" massacre months earlier by the U.S. forces. There was a lot of commotion still in the air when I arrived for my first infantry assignment to be sent into the neighboring villages and jungles to police the area. Keep in mind, even though I wasn't aware in the beginning of all the enemies I was about to encounter, my enemies were aware of me!

Charlie along with Alpha, Bravo and Delta companies made up our battalion. The way the soldiers were managed in Charlie Company was in the following fashion: a company contained approximately 200 men called troops, who were divided into four platoons each containing four squads, each squad had eight to twelve persons. "C" or Charlie Company had a captain assigned as the C.O. or commanding officer in charge of all four platoons. Each platoon usually had a lieutenant as its leader. Each squad had a "squad leader" usually a sergeant who assigned each one in that squad with their individual duties. Each squad featured a machine gunner with an ammo carrier, one grenadier, one radio-telephone-operator or RTO, sometimes a medic, sometimes a dog, sometimes a Vietnamese scout and all others. All others carried rifles, ammo, grenades, bayonet, a backpack carrying: food, water, poncho, poncho liner and entrenching shovel, which in total weighed from 50 to 75 pounds. All wore a steel pot helmet, helmet liner, or bush hat, a protective frag-jacket, clothing called fatigues (no wonder I always was tired), and jungle combat boots.

Well here I was preparing to go to the jungle for the first time in my first week all dressed up in the full battle array mentioned above. It was more like the first day of football practice for a person who had never put on a helmet, shoulder-pads, hip-pads, thigh-pads, knee-pads and rounded it out with high top football cleats. It took time to acclimate and balance all you were carrying along with the weight on your back. You couldn't run without being clumsy. You couldn't walk without feeling awkward. Throw in the heat and you were miserable and hot most of the time. Finally toss in all the fables, facts, fictions and fears the guys who had been there awhile told you and you were all set to move out against the enemy, right? Not!

The helicopters (nicknamed "choppers") arrived and as always hurried in to pick us up fully equipped, take us to our assignment and then hurried out. They were always more vulnerable targets for the enemy if they would not hustle. For 99 percent of us new guys it was our first helicopter ride. The ride wasn't so bad. The unknown destiny that awaited us ruined any sense of enjoying our first flight. As soon as our door gunner started opening up by shooting his machine gun at the hillside where the colored smoke grenades had clouded the area, all the door gunners in the fleet then in unison began firing in deafening harmony. The pilot shouted, while the helicopter was now hovering over a muddy swamp, "jump out here right now, I can't land, it's a hot landing zone!" It was only about eight feet to the ground, but with all the weight I carried when I jumped I stuck in the mud to my above my knees. "Great, I thought, I'm going to get shot on my first day stuck in the mud without firing a shot! What a heroic soldier I am!" There was some return fire that soon dissipated. I made it out of the mud with a little help from my buddies or better said-muddies.

A little later while I was cleaning up the mud from my pants and boots, I noticed I had some uninvited visitors. They were attached to my legs. Black, slimy, blood-sucking leeches! No, I'm not cussing. I'm not talking about Robin Leech of the "Rich and Famous!" These little critters, called leeches, were constantly attaching themselves to body parts. We had to stop every hour wherever they propagated and had to strip down for a "leech" check. In some cases they attached themselves to places I can't mention. Thank God for the "bug juice" we carried with us to kill them, the ticks, and all the other miniature armies of insects and pests. Every day we had to deal with mosquitoes that could bite through clothing and pierce skin. I think the enemy must have issued them bayonets. Daily we had to take our big Orange pill and little White pill to prevent malaria. I became so used to bugs, spiders and crawling things that even during sleep, when a huge cockroach was under my shirt overrunning my chest hair, I would simply smash them as they popped. Sounds gross, I know, but just what would you do, prissy? Every morning a giant horsefly with a buzz saw would wake you up. There was an even distribution of horsefly alarms, one per tent. Another lovely benefit of camping out! Do you see now why I answered the question on my initial entrance exam regarding if I enjoyed camping out with an emphatic NO? My first air lift, my first day, my first leech, my new insect pets, what excitement was to follow later tonight? *

CHAPTER 9

A NIGHT TO REMEMBER

Before nightfall and before every night thereafter we would first routinely set up a perimeter defense. Sometimes we would dig out foxholes for cover if we were in areas highly exposed and likely to receive incoming mortar fire. At other times, when we were hidden in dense jungle, that wouldn't be necessary. We would find sticks or pieces of bamboo and pitch a tent with two ponchos connected together, put them over the sticks and tie them down with stakes. It was then time to blow up our air mattresses and later go to sleep if we didn't have guard watch that night.

After finishing putting up the tent we would sit down for a nice hot supper. Nice? Well, would you believe hot? We would take out one box of C-rations from our backpack and open it up with the following contents: one can of your favorite meal; one good old pr-25 can-opener; one small can of petrified crackers; some cheese to hide the taste of the crackers; one small can of dry, World War II peanut butter; some jelly; a piece of undesirable, hockey-puck chocolate; a bag of cocoa mix; one heating tab to be set under the can of the main dish, I meant main can; some matches; a bag with napkin, eating utensils, salt and pepper, and of course a small bundle of ever so precious toilet paper! Imagine all of this in one small box for your eating pleasure. Of course you have a variety of exciting choices for your main dish/can. For example, my favorite was tuna loaf well burnt. I had to pass on the ham and lima beans, if you catch my drift. The novelty of eating these meals ended after one week. It was time to diet. It's not that I wasn't thankful for having food, it was just that my taste buds had been spoiled for the meals back home. Every day we would talk of a smothered, green chile, beef and bean burrito or spaghetti with sausage and meatballs covered with Parmesan cheese and Italian bread or a steak or mom's Sunday roast with mashed potatoes and gravy. Of course that only made it worse. Never mind mama's cooking? Where's mama?

After dining and before going to bed or taking your turn at guard duty, the most entertaining time of the day was the night time conversation where we would gather and talk about the craziness of the day and how we felt about everything. This is the time we would wind down, release our frustrations, get sentimental or philosophical and express ourselves to the friends we chose to relate to. It was healthy to have somebody to share your heart with. On the other hand, if a person had no one to relate to it made the days more unbearable. All the questions concerning life, death, war, God, family, wives, kids, pain, health, the future, the present, the past and the people we were involved with in this circumstance were the daily popular subjects. There wasn't much wisdom available due to the inexperience of the young men, yet it still was a release mechanism. It was during these times we grew and matured in character, understanding and bonding.

I remember before going to bed one night I was watching our medic, named Fisher, later called Doc, finish digging a foxhole. I liked Doc Fisher, an Afro-American from northern California, who never carried a rifle due to his religious beliefs as a conscientious objector yet served faithfully as a good medic. He was digging away with his entrenching tool. That small shovel took so much effort in digging a fox hole scarcely big enough for a fox let alone a person. Doc was taking every precaution to protect his life as a husband and father that he felt was necessary. We were currently in a wide-open area on top of a hill and were warned that we could be vulnerable to a mortar attack. As I looked at the small hole he dug, I laughed at Fisher as I quipped, "Doc, do you honestly think this hole is big enough for you to jump into if we were really under mortar fire?" He confidently replied, "Yep!"

No sooner had Fisher said yep, a horrible whistling sound followed by a tremendous thundering cracking explosion literally shook the ground we were standing on like an earthquake. It was a mortar attack! Fisher immediately jumped in the ever so small hole he had dug. By sheer reflex and fear I jumped in on top of him. The crazy thing was there was still room above my back below ground level. We were scared out of our wits. As the mortars went off one by one and shook our hill we felt so helpless in protecting ourselves. We started praying together, "God please don't let one of these bombs hit on top of us!" The old adage, "There are no atheists in a foxhole," never proved to be more true. We scarcely had room enough to move or breathe but we managed to laugh inside that foxhole after the attack finally subsided. "Doc, I have to apologize to you, I said, for not trusting your expertise in excavation! Thanks for saving my life!" He just laughed in satisfaction and relief. Neither one of us could believe we had both fit like contortionists into that hole as we stood now above it. Either the concussion or the flying shrapnel that came with the mortar attack could have killed anyone caught above ground. My prayer life had now just begun kick-started by mortar fire. I knew I was only mortal that day and could use help from a higher, stronger source. My faith and belief system shifted into high gear that day. From that day on Doc and I became closer friends. If I had the ability or the means I wouldn't let anything or anybody come to harm him and would put my life on the line for him if ever necessary. We agreed that one-day we would have to tell our kids the story about the day when two men became close friends inside a foxhole. I love you Doc, thanks!*

CHAPTER 10

TENESSEE GOES HOME

THERE WAS THIS one day I was in a bad mood. I'll tell the truth, my attitude stunk! It was a hot, muggy, miserable Monday walking who knew where. I'm not sure why I even had to tell you it was Monday since all the days seemed to be the same. It's not like we had the weekends off or holidays either. As a matter of fact it was just like most every other day with the exception of my bad attitude. Have you ever sensed that this was just not going to be a good day? Well that day I did.

As was the custom, the entire company was walking single file towards our latest village destination. In "guerilla" warfare, which was much different than the "front line" combat featured in the previous World Wars, we would be safest when we were all spread out and not in a cluster. Our most common encounters with snipers hidden everywhere required us not to gather to allow the sniper easy targets. Likewise, the hidden mines and booby traps called for us to walk in single file, spread out so that the least amount of damage would occur from the shrapnel that flew everywhere 360 degrees.

Always dangerous and tedious was the assignment when a platoon or a squad had to walk "point." Point simply was the first soldier in line leading the entire company, platoon or squad. The point man had the responsibility to watch for any irregularities in the ground or dirt that could possibly be a mine or booby-trap and then communicate to the guy behind him to keep passing any information down the line. In jungle conditions the point man or point squad who led had to use machetes to cut a path through the dense jungle vegetation and vines, called "wait-a-minute vines," because they would grab everything possible and hold you up a moment until you could break loose. This was not a desirable job to anyone but nevertheless was necessary.

"Look out for this, watch out for that, don't step on that, be careful of that, step over this, be careful of this," were the words that were repeated two hundred times at every unhealthy sign on the ground, to our flank or above as they were passed down the single file of soldiers. These were the words you heard all day, every day, as we moved on foot. In the beginning I would make sure that every step I took would be in the footprint of the person before me. That was the way one could be sure he did not trigger a mine. The footprint before you insured you that your next step was safe. We would all be cautiously looking down like hunchbacks, never really paying much attention to the scenery but focusing on not being blown up that day. It became so monotonous and miserable walking in that manner in the heat of the day and we didn't dare walk in the night where we couldn't see the ground if it had been tampered with. When we were hot, tired, and miserable we would often get lazy and even careless, quit looking down, not communicate and not follow the footprints in front of you. At times we even quit caring. It was usually those times when something bad happened.

As I mentioned earlier, at the conclusion of each day we would discuss today's futility along with our dreams of freedom in our nightly conversations. Most everyone had a "nickname." Some of the pet names were friendly labels of endearment, some were terms of sarcasm. I called my squad leader Wally (Sergeant Moon) because he looked like a muscle bound version of Wally from "Leave it to Beaver." We got along real well. He was a good soldier and I learned a lot on how to survive in the "bush" from him. There was another guy named "Animal." This was due to the fact he never bathed, shaved or got a hair cut. One day Animal was approached by a full bird colonel (can you tell me why this is pronounced currr'—nel?) who just landed by helicopter in the middle of a jungle excursion. He looked at Animal, took his rifle and examined it and because he smelled so bad and because his rifle had rust on it he was given an Article 15, a fine, and lost one stripe in rank.

One of the funniest characters was a guy they called "Hillbilly." He feared nothing. Someone thought they saw a sniper in a clump of bushes so Hillbilly ran right in that direction and jumped into the bushes. Thank God no one was in those bushes. He later shot a NVA paymaster with a hunk of piasters (Vietnamese money) and bought the whole company Coca Colas. "German" was the strange name for a strange guy who ate lizards. Thus went the nicknames for the variety of people from all parts of the world and diverse backgrounds who came together to serve in the U. S. Army. Another guy's name was Tennessee. He got that name because he was from Louisiana and we didn't want to call him Louise. Just kidding, he was an old-fashioned good old boy from Tennessee. I can still remember his black curly hair, his great jovial laughing smile as his eyes squinted. He was just a friendly likeable guy. One of the things I enjoyed was to get to know an individual. One of the downfalls in war, on the other hand in getting too close to an individual, was when you have to deal with the trauma of loss of that person you now held in your heart. Tennessee would tell us of his dreams of one day going to Nashville and one day singing on the Grand 'Ole Opera. We would have him sing some of our favorite country western songs to his own twang style. That man could sing! He was gifted, that is if you appreciated country music. He had a future like many of us if he would only survive this war. I remember once he had told us that if he ever stepped on a mine to just tie a tourniquet, cut off his leg and send him home. I learned you have to be careful what you say, what you believe and what you ask for.

Well as I was saying earlier we all were walking in single file when all of a sudden a huge explosion went off about one hundred yards behind me that miserable attitudinal day. What had happened? They sent the news up to us, "it was a land mine, it got Tennessee." Every tragedy happened so quickly, that it usually was over before you had any chance to change the circumstance. The medical evacuation helicopter soon arrived within ten minutes. I was there to see him before they carried him aboard. He was visibly shook, intermittently crying in fear of losing his leg and said, "cut if off so I won't die." He was the first of many I would later see wounded or shot and evacuated. Cold reality struck as the news came back the next day that he had lost his foot from the ankle down but was going to be O.K. A shock wave went into the heart of every man who knew and felt bad for him and his family, thinking, "this also could have been me." One more heart "hit" for all who knew him. The only good news that day was that Tennessee was going home.*

CHAPTER 11

MY FIRST AMBUSH, SHORT OF HEROIC

It was inevitable that one day I was going to confront Charlie face to face, live and in person. We were told that sometime that week we were going out on a full company mission again into the jungles. It was time for me to go the barbershop and to get a haircut and have my ears lowered. We were allowed to go the stores and shops close-by during the day before night curfew. Of course the merchants were all Vietnamese citizens. The barber who gave me a haircut also gave me a shave this time with a leather-sharpened razor. I looked real good that day but nobody cared, except me. I went back to the complex that day, business as usual.

Two days later, I was given guard duty the same evening on the border perimeter of our base camp. The perimeter was heavily surrounded with constertina (spelling?) wire, similar to thickly rolled barbed wire. Each night we would put our claymore mines out just inside the wire, hook them up to the wiring device and proceed to have guard watch. This went on every night with soldiers spread out the entire 360 degrees of our perimeter. Well, the obvious happened! One claymore mine abruptly exploded followed by machine gun and rifle fire and simultaneous flares to light up the entire area like an array of fireworks. It was clamorous and tremulous to say the least. When all the noise had subsided we continued our guard until the break of day. That morning upon further inspection of the damage and enemy casualties the outcome of the final survey proved to be a Viet Cong sapper attack. The proof was lying dead in black pajamas caught in the middle of our wire border. "Gi" (pronounced j-eye), a citizen of Chu Lai, our 15 year old Vietnamese scout, recognized and identified all those killed that night. The biggest shock that came from the identification was that one of the men killed in the wire was my barber! That gave me the creeps and sent a chill throughout my body to think that same man I had trusted with a razor at my neck two days earlier could have killed me in the barber chair and was then trying to kill me that night. I'm glad I didn't tip him! Never settle for cheap haircuts. It could cost you. Like I asked earlier, "Who is the enemy?"

By the end of that week we were airlifted away from our base, squad by squad, helicopter after helicopter, to a distant bunkered- complex. From there each platoon was given a territory to search, police, and report back after setting up an ambush at the end of the day to determine any movement of the enemy. Each night one squad from each platoon was to walk about five miles from the base hub to eventually cover the entire five-mile circular radius. Tonight was my squad's turn to go out and it was my first time to set an ambush. I was extremely nervous preparing to walk that distance away from the safety and protection of our company's firepower. Of course your imagination runs wild to think that you might be overpowered by a larger number of soldiers. One by one in single file we walked in each other's footprints for five miles through rice paddies and weeds until we reached our designated destination. We radioed in our grid coordinates according to our map assignment so we would be covered on all sides by 105-millimeter artillery in case we were outnumbered or being overrun. Each phosphorous, artillery round safely surrounded us and marked our position, as we called in the artillery and walked the rounds within our protective radius. One of the rounds hit a baboon or large monkey in the distance and it cried in pain like a human baby for hours.

Alternating, we each took a turn sleeping one hour while the others stayed awake vigilant prepared to ambush anything or anyone that confronted us. After my first watch it was my turn to take an hour nap about two in the morning. So sleepily I unsnapped my frag-jacket for comfort as I lay down on my back. I placed my steel pot helmet close to my left hand and I placed my M-16 rifle inches away from my right hand. If anything happened, so I figured, I would just put on my helmet, pick up my rifle and begin to fire away. A few minutes into my short nap, moving figures were approaching our ambush site. First the machine gun opened up and burst into action and every weapon we had then let loose immediately. My plan to put on my helmet and grab my rifle coming out of a sleep defaulted to clumsily grabbing everywhere for them in the dark. It seemed to take me five minutes before I was coordinated enough to fire my rifle. I unloaded magazine after magazine of bullets shot in the general direction of a target I never really saw, which meant I couldn't tell if I hit anything in the dark shadows of the night. Within fifteen minutes the ambush had taken its toll. From sleep to fear, from fear to adrenaline and then back to fear went my emotions. We stayed up wide-awake until the break of dawn. Before dawn we radioed back to the base when they called after hearing all the noise of our weapon barrage. They asked for a body count and assessment of the damage as soon as we could see in daylight.*

CHAPTER 12

DEATH REARS ITS UGLY HEAD

The spirit of "Death" saturated the air moving about as a dark, eerie, slowly slithering presence. It was discernibly tangible, something I never felt before, but sensed its cold chill and invisible stench. The awareness multiplied when we found the bodies of three dead women sprawled and contorted as they lay dead in the weeds, never to see a sunrise again. As my mind took mental snapshots of these deceased human beings, the reality of the moment was overbearing. I couldn't process the entire scene all at once. These possibly were just farmers going out to the fields early as they did every other day not heeding the curfew of the war regulations. They could be Viet Cong running nocturnal reconnaissance, however that was unlikely. My mind couldn't go there but defaulted to seeing only dead women, probably someone's mom, somebody's daughter, or possibly somebody's wife. What a tragedy! What a waste! To come to an ending of one's life like this was a disgrace to human dignity, war's ever so common consequence.

Experiencing the trauma of death, killing, murder, and the like will change a person forever. The pictures of that first episode have been contained in my heart's memory almost 40 years later. When I had to identify the sex of the dead persons, I treated that like they were made only of rubber, not flesh and blood, so I could somehow process the reality. My job in our squad at the time was the RTO (Radio-Telephone Operator) since I could communicate well over the radio. I was at a loss for words that day. We had encountered at least seven people in the ambush that night by the sheer evidence that there were seven sets of straw hats and slippers, three of which were close to the deceased. If there was more than that, they either got away free or as was their custom just tied a tourniquet around the wounded limb and ran to hiding.

From that day on I witnessed many more fatalities including those of our own soldiers. Now I had realized I actually had left the former reality of a world I had known and entered into a new realm, in a way, a new manner of existence, to which I so slowly yet subtly had to accept. Every hour seemed to pass as if I was proceeding in a surreal slow-motion frame as to highlight and emphasize each new experience. This new environment now had tainted my thought life, heightened my emotional life and changed my overall paradigm and perception of what I used to think life was all about. Each traumatic event left an indelible mark on my heart's memory. Now I had been fully absorbed into a whole new culture with all new friends whose common denominator was to help each other survive this landscape. The spirit of Death became a constant, undesirable companion, lurking about always in the background like a serpent, just waiting for its cue and permission for its next appearance and opportunity. I never had to look for it consciously and its overture and presence continued to harden me on the inside so that I would be able to tolerate it. The fear of my death became a constant reminder of its ultimate toll and purpose, a fear of final abandonment much like a laughing hyena ever haunting and tormenting me. We were not trained to release all these feelings and emotions caused by death's experience ever so close and discernible. Instead, we just bottled them up, held on to them until one day the pressure cooker would have to blow. If this isn't the definition of trauma, how else could the reader explain, that since 1970, I am still able to recall all these things so accurately and with such detail? How then were we to ever escape or erase this reality? We were 10,000 miles away from home without any means to leave. Would there ever be a solution to conquer this spirit of fear that constantly was oppressing us? My heart was looking again for answers to these questions so that I could at least endure this emotional combat from one day to the next. What could I do to desensitize myself? *+

CHAPTER 13

DRUGS—ONE MEANS OF TEMPORARY ESCAPE

War has many by-products and pollutants, most of which are not beneficial to man or living things. War unleashes so many evils that I can only attempt to list some of them. It literally opens up Pandora's box of moral depravity. When I was first exposed to the spirit of death, initiated by the killings that took place in my first ambush, there emerged the temptation offering a perverted license to take down all moral barriers, all ethical codes which up to that point, had kept each individual in check within its legal restrictions. Killing releases lawlessness and its many exhibitions and forms that had been hidden and once dormant in the heart of man. Now that former sleeping giant appeared. Some of those evils I will spare the reader even the mention of the contaminated, perverted events that

I witnessed which were atrocities to humanity and the very dignity of a civilized world. Even though I could give graphic details of some of the combat scenes I witnessed, the purpose for writing this book would not be served. These only expanded the depth of emotional trauma. The mentality in wartime defaulted to the conclusion that if killing, life's greatest enemy is now allowed, all other evil things couldn't be worse and therefore why not also be permitted? Unfortunately this thinking eludes rational logic and becomes par for all wars, where almost anything goes.

One hideous plague that has carried its seemingly incurable disease even to this present day and to our own home court was the selling, buying and use of drugs. It became a thriving industry during the Viet Nam era. The returning soldiers transferred the outbreak of this disease back home to the U.S. and to several other countries. Many people were introduced to drugs of all kinds for the first time in their lives during this period in history, as were those in-country. We of Charlie Company were no exception. The Vietnamese people smoked marijuana daily as part of their routine cultural lifestyle. They would sell us a shopping bag full of "weed" at the bargain price of one dollar. Soldiers would write home or catalogue mail order for electric blenders to make the marijuana more pleasant and smokeable. It became a common thing to have it in your possession even during battle conditions. It was to some a means of escaping and numbing the fear and torment of the frigid reality of this war. Later it might have even progressed to an addiction, a co-dependency, and a source of temporary peace and welcomed its medicine for withdrawal from everything to which we were being subjected.

One soldier named "K" was very heavy into that drug's influence. He smoked "pot" every day in secret and was always well supplied. In the middle of the day during a company operation he was walking around as usual very much under its influence. As he walked preoccupied and not paying any attention to the eminent danger beneath his feet, all of a sudden a mine, like a thief, took from him both of his legs as it violently exploded beneath. "K" was immediately evacuated by helicopter back to the rear to the hospital in an attempt to save him from bleeding to death. Routinely we had to send all personal belongings back to our base camp when one was injured. In his back pack food pouch we found no food at all because it was completely filled up with marijuana. We hid that fact from the officers in charge. Later that day, our Captain went to visit "K" in the hospital to see how he was doing. Our C.O. told us that when he asked "K", "what had happened?" and if he was O.K., "K" only could say, "Wow! What can I say?" Wow was his favorite saying and we knew by his response that he was still high on grass but low on life span and with little chance of a future.

Drugs spurred the increase of a growing "Black Market" money business. The buying and selling of drugs kept the flow of money steady which in turn kept the Black Market economy alive and healthy. U.S. greenback dollars were constantly being exchanged at a higher rate and value for piasters, the currency of Viet Nam, and M.P.C., the U.S. military payment currency. The Black Market thrived on soldier greenbacks being illegally traded in for the multiplication of M.P.C. Now that market was sending our U.S. money into other countries. That same money was also used for the exchange for other material goods, military weapons, sex, drugs and whatever else you can think of buying. This gave birth to the drug traffic we find in many countries today and initiated some of the drug cartels that presently are active and making a living on killing human beings with its addictions. You can thank war for its contribution to today's drug dominance over the human spirit, which now has reached an epidemic level and is growing at an almost unstoppable pace.

Once upon a time I was offered a piece of carrot cake one evening that had been laced with opium by some nurses. They said it was kind of like "Alice B. Toklas" brownies that were baked with marijuana. I loved home-made sweets and so I figured, "What harm would a little opium in a beautiful piece of carrot cake do?" Well it did no harm to me, that is, for at least the first thirty minutes afterwards. I consumed that delicious piece of cake wholeheartedly as usual not expecting anything that was about to happen. Then my first & only opium "trip" began. First I got paranoid much like a drunk looking to gain his equilibrium and was looking for relief by eating something to gain back some semblance of control. Frantically, I started for the NCO club to get something to eat. I started down the stairs of the back door of the barracks and as I was walking now ever so bouncy in my tennis shoes, my strides had become gigantic leaps. I hallucinated that I had started to grow in size much like Gulliver in the land of Lilliput and now towered over the diminutive buildings. The stars and the light of the moon were flashing and dancing with me with each colossal step. Just ask Alice when she was ten feet tall! I reached the NCO club and immediately went into the restroom out of conditioned response. I went to the sink, turned on the cold water and clumsily splashed my face while trying to come out of this twilight zone as I pinched and slapped my face to wake up. After all, I had some practice before trying to wake myself up from a bad dream. I don't remember how or what I said to order some food but could remember eating some chicken. I stuffed a chicken drumstick in my mouth and immediately pulled out only the bones. I did this over and over until I had to leave to go to somewhere else so I could recover from this. This episode gave a new meaning to surreal.

My friends, who had given me the cake and who had experience in getting "high", thoroughly enjoyed watching me carry on the way I did. While they laughed and laughed, I was getting madder and madder and said, "This is not funny at all. How do I come out of this?" One guy said, "Here, just take some gum and chew it. It will help." "Why not, I thought, any cure if it will help." As I chewed the gum my mouth and lower jaw got bigger and bigger and went lower and lower until I imagined my jaw hitting the floor where I was sitting. "I gotta get outta here," I said. Next I tried the only remedy I could think of, trying to sleep it off. As I lie down to close my eyes, though the bed didn't start turning in circles like in my alcohol experiences, it did elevate somewhat. My last fearful sentiment before finally falling to sleep was, "I'm never going to come out of this drugged state but if I do I'll never do that again!"

In the morning I reluctantly opened my eyes, afraid it still wasn't over. It was! Thank God! I hated everything associated with that trip. Not one moment of that high did I enjoy, instead I spent the entire time in fear with the discomfort of not being in control of myself. Luckily that one bad experience cured me of ever wanting to do any kind of drugs, whether marijuana, LSD, opium or the like. I did however come to the conclusion that this form of departure from reality to an altered state of consciousness was an experience many encountered and many carried home with them never overcoming the addiction. It was a doorway to eventually try stronger drugs. Another spiritual battleground had been revealed and another enemy was introduced, called drugs, and they joined the cast of this drama. This drug avenue was obviously not going to be my solution for finding peace or sanity but shortly thereafter the solution was going to show up. *

CHAPTER 14

MY FIRST GOOD "SPIRITUAL ENCOUNTER"

I HAVE TO apologize for the last three chapters you have read. Admittedly they have been gloomy and depressing to say the least. Try to understand that whenever I have to recall those incidents from stored heart memory, the negativity and emotional darkness that surface simply were the sentiments I was feeling at that time. That is why a lot of returning soldiers don't like to repeat much of their war experience. The recollection remains too vivid of the past and they are trying to forget and heal emotionally. Why dig up what you are trying to bury? Besides, no one except those who had like experiences would really understand anyway. The reason I'm able to share this today after so many years have passed is because of what I'm about to tell you. I also apologize for my sarcastic attitude.

Whenever I would be involved in a firefight with the enemy or pinned down by sniper fire, the first thing I would do was pray. I was raised a Catholic and I was a believer in Jesus Christ and my faith always had me aware that somehow God was going to help me through all of this. I can't remember a single moment when I doubted His existence or ability to help should He choose to do so. At the time I only knew prayers that I was taught to pray at home and in school and in church. So, being a Catholic, I wore a rosary around my neck along with a peace sign and chain. My favorite prayer was the "Act of Contrition." I said it every time I thought I was going to die.

During one day's jungle operation we were just sitting around and resting after walking a few miles. Four of us were playing a card game called, "Acey-Duecey" with a good pile of money in the pot. All of a sudden sniper shots rudely interrupted the game. Of all the nerve! I still remember and still can see that scene. We all hit the ground and low crawled to cover so fast that I was ready to shoot before the cards and the money, which we threw up into the air and were in a slow motion freeze frame floating still, hit the ground. I started praying sincerely as always, "O my God, I am heartily sorry for having offended Thee and I detest all my sins because I dread the loss of heaven and the pains of hell. But most of all because I offend Thee my God who art all good and deserving of all my love. I truly resolve with the help of Thy grace to sin no

more and to avoid the near occasions of sin. Amen."
(Act of Contrition)

After saying that little prayer my faith assured me my sins were forgiven as I prepared myself for whatever came next, even death should I feel its sting. You would be surprised how sincere and real your prayers become in the middle of combat. You either believe them or not. This time something happened on the inside of me I couldn't explain but could only measure it by feeling peace that followed. For the first time in my life, as I was facing possible death, I felt a peaceful resolve to embrace life or death, should this be my final curtain call. My faith had overcome my fear. Don't misunderstand me. It was still very tense during the skirmish but I was working through it with a new motivation, a newly found strength, faith not fear, faith that God was with me.

That was my first encounter as a believer of a protective God that was up close and present that gave me a feeling I was no longer alone but He was defending me. My constant companion, the fear of abandonment, no longer resided in my heart. This new strength grew day by day and upon confrontation after confrontation. It now had taken up residency where fear used to abide. Finally it settled in my heart and now in my thought life. Faith to live now became what I believed and thus I spoke. I now confessed to everyone out loud, "I'm not going to die here and I'm not going to be harmed. I'm getting out of here with both legs, both arms, and anyone I'm with will not be hurt either, for my God is with me." Some believed and followed. Let the records show this statement proved to be true.

Unfortunately the protection I now felt wasn't the case for some. As I looked about a hundred yards towards the sun to the west I saw people strangely jumping up high into the air. A cloud of dust followed and then the sound of a huge explosion reached our ears. Someone had been blown up into the air by another mine. Who could it have been this time? Word came quickly that it was our platoon leader, our lieutenant. He and the first platoon leader, both lieutenants had been investigating what they thought might be a mine. Before the demolition squad came to diffuse the mine, one of the Vietnamese scouts ran and jumped on it in a final suicide maneuver. The lieutenants had both legs blown off and were immediately rushed by helicopter to the hospital. That's the last time we saw the two of them and the last time anyone would see them alive. There was such a requiem silence the next couple of days. When you lose your leader that suddenly, whom you had admired and befriended, you don't know which emotion to employ. The spirit of fear of death, of course, immediately took up residence as it came into our camp along with sadness, compassion, and pity for the families who were going to get the bad news at their door read by soldiers in full dress uniforms. Each time something like this happened you have to suck it up, stuff it in and deal with it eventually. There was no counseling available. The favorite saying after a tragedy was, "It just don't mean nothing." Bad English, I know, but it was our way of not dealing with it emotionally and writing it off. Just suck it up! Suck it up! What's that?

Our lieutenant was a good man, a great dad and a loving husband. This I knew because of how lovingly he would show me the pictures of his child and his wife that was about to give birth. Each night he prayed for his family as he frequently spoke of them. We all took time to write letters to his wife to tell of our admiration of her husband and our leader. It still makes me sad to think that he had to die that way. What a terrible loss and waste of goodness. His wife in turn sent our platoon a letter in reply and said he had written to her about us and how proud he was to lead some of the bravest men he had ever met. When I heard those words, I broke down in tears. I did it again right now as I wrote this to you. I hadn't had to tell anyone about this until I wrote this book. I guess I'll never really understand why the good guys with the white hats die just like the bad guys with black hats because obviously war is not a respecter of persons. I never did blame God, like some did, for not protecting the lieutenant the same way He was protecting me because I knew He didn't start this war, people did! This was a clear case of God giving man dominion over planet earth and man abusing that dominion by his own free will in making poor decisions. (In memory of 1st lieutenant Gary Mower and family.) *

CHAPTER 15

MANY "CLOSE CALLS"

It was now no longer the roll of the dice or Lady Luck that determined my fate but rather the right hand of Almighty God. It became my new confidence like a warm blanket continually protecting my consciousness with its comfortable embrace. Each night after the death of the lieutenants we would gather together as usual and have our discussions, however, now the debates were filled with much controversy. Questioning these last weeks had escalated to more spiritual considerations. Now there were sincere questions regarding life and death, heaven and hell, God or no God, mortality and immortality. We kept arriving closer to some of the answers but not ones that fully satisfied our most curious inquisitiveness. We would walk away each night with those thoughts to consider during our sleep.

I'd like to tell you all the "close calls" with death I had since my first encounter with God but I'll list a few just to make my point. Just minutes after I said that Act of Contrition at the outset of the sniper attack it was quickly over. I had blindly emptied my magazines in the direction of the sound of the sniper's shots. In my youth I watched many war movies and concluded, "If I were ever in the line of fire, I would keep my head down so they wouldn't have my face as a target." I wasn't one so curious that I would get up just to see where the enemy was. I simply shot into the general vicinity of the noise. Remember this is not a story of a war hero. Audie Murphy would never have been challenged by my combat performance. From the area into which I shot came three of our own soldiers in my direction. A huge sigh of relief came after I realized I could have killed my own team. They were filling up canteens with water fifty yards in front of me. It was a wonderful thing that both they kept down and that I was a bad shot. Thank you, Jesus!

We were fighting for the freedom of Democracy. At the time I didn't really understand the depth of that principle of government by the people. You don't appreciate that until you see all those fighting for it. We had it "made in the shade" back home. Freedom was taken for granted and even the freedom to be stupid. Letters from loved ones were always welcomed more than gold or silver and back flashed us to our homes that now seemed so far away. Newspapers and magazines would give us details of the war picketing and demonstrations at the universities of those opposing the war. On one hand I appreciated those that were trying to influence the end of the war but on the other hand we felt the hatred from those who criticized the soldiers being there. Adding the current character of President Richard Nixon to this equation of confusion and sometimes we felt better off here. There was no safe place on the planet it seemed. You either deal with the given reality or hide. The letters from home and memories kept you diverted at times but then all of a sudden...

One evening while we were going out to set up another ambush, we sat down for a rest in a shallow ravine. As I was day dreaming about home, machine gun fire with green tracers flew over our heads. We dropped down to our backs and lay close to the ground. I could have raised my hand and touched the dotted line of bullets as the tracers indicated the enemy's position. It's was a fortunate thing the trajectory was in a straight line since it couldn't cover depressions in the earth. Later that same week we were walking through a cornfield and machine gun fire dug up the dirt right next to us. There was nowhere to hide as I hit the ground between the cornrows next to the dirt holding up the corn. When you are under attack you try to become as small as possible and get as close to the ground as possible so that you might become knee high to a grasshopper. Missed me, again! Luck? Maybe! Divine Intervention? Most likely!

We were airlifted one time to search the Ho Chi Min trail for potential rocket attacks during the TET Offensive celebration. Did I mention we were dropped illegally into Cambodia, into the DMZ (demilitarized zone)? We found a cache of over fifteen rockets positioned by the enemy on bamboo tripods accurately aimed and targeted for the Chu Lai ammo dump and motor pool. By the way, I thank God for the Air Force with their air support, the Navy for their artillery and gun power from the sea, and the Marines who had the nastiest job of all securing hot spots. Thank you all for helping keep us alive! We immediately called for a napalm strike, which systematically blew up the enemy's hidden rockets. These rockets were so heavy two Vietnamese soldiers had to carry one for miles on their shoulders to that destination. We didn't feel bad ruining their 4th of July fireworks display. Before the strike we retreated for cover to what we thought was a safe distance. As the napalm explosions destroyed the rockets, I kneeled down to lace my right combat boot. A piece of hot burning metal shrapnel the size of a Frisbee landed six inches from my boot with the thud of a bowling ball as it kicked up the dirt. Once again I deeply sighed in relief to think it could have seared my flesh and bones and totally ruined my day. Another close-call!

On another occasion sergeant Wally and I were sharing perimeter guard watch after the point platoon shot a NVA soldier during a company march down a river. As is their custom, the Vietnamese will always come to retrieve their dead as soon as they thought it would be safe to do so. Knowing that, our company used the body as a decoy and set up trip wires around it. The trip wires were designed both to set off a claymore mine and to ignite flares so those holding watch could hear the bang, see the lighted area and proceed to shoot the ones coming back for the body. Wally, as was his personal custom, would hold watch with a grenade in one hand and the index finger of the other hand inside the grenade's firing pin. He told me that in case he fell asleep and heard something coming at us he would pull the pin and throw it. Well that was almost a good idea.

The trip wires worked. The bang of the claymore mine worked. The flares lit up the night's darkness. There was one problem with the plan. It woke up Wally from a deep nap. You see he didn't usually fall asleep on watch but since we were in triple canopy jungle that had nothing but trees, trees and more trees surrounded by dense vegetation, he figured no one was going to bother us in the night by tripping through the darkness. Now the real problem was when Wally woke up, he pulled the pin and threw the grenade. Normally that wouldn't be any problem except for the tree that it hit with a thud was only five feet away. He said, "Scheck take cover!" I couldn't move anywhere in the remaining 10 seconds or less that it takes a grenade to explode, so I just grabbed my helmet and lay flat on my stomach prostrate. BANG! It exploded right next to us. When it went off, Wally hurriedly asked me if I was O.K. I answered, "yes, are you?" He said, "I'm O.K., it didn't hit me." When the bang went off, someone yelled, "Incoming!" They thought that bang came from outside our perimeter so the entire company opened fire and proceeded to shoot every weapon available including calling in for artillery into the grids we had set up for that night. It was estimated somewhere around $50,000 worth of fireworks that were discharged because of that grenade. Once again both I and the person next to me were protected. Wally said, "Don't tell anyone about this." I said I wouldn't if he wouldn't. Wally, I didn't until now!

One night while sleeping I was bit by a scorpion. It stung me and I proceeded to smash it and go back to sleep. The next day my left hip had a nasty swelling where I was stung but I just continued on like normal. The second day the swelling increased and there were red lines extending from the bite down to my knee. I still didn't feel too bad but it sure wasn't looking good. The third day I showed Doc the bite because now I was getting lock-jaw from its poison and had difficulty opening my mouth to talk. He said it looked like blood poisoning, a layman's term for infection, so he sent me in on the next helicopter going back to the base so a doctor could look at it.

That trip to the hospital proved to be not only fortuitous but also divinely providential. The doctor hooked me to an I.V. to get my strength back and an antibiotic to fight the scorpion toxin. He lanced the open sore and drained and cleaned the area. Because of the high humidity he couldn't stitch it up right away but had to wait to see if it was healing properly. Meanwhile, since I had to stay there for seven days, news came back that our company was being hit by a full size NVA army. I felt bad that they were under attack but I didn't feel bad that I was absent. When I told two sergeants that I was glad to be here and not there, one of them called me a "chicken." Why, them's fighting words! So I said, "We'll see who's a chicken" as one sergeant proceeded to punch me right in the nose. I retaliated by punching him in the nose and so also the other sergeant who came at me after I punched his friend. The result—three punches landed—three noses broken and several black eyes. The only reason they didn't put me in jail is because one hit me first. They did later apologize, however, and said that I wasn't a chicken. One of the sergeants remarked, "I've been here in Viet Nam for an entire year with no injuries or wounds and now that I have one week left before I go home, I gotta go home with a face like this, thanks to you, Scheck." The atmosphere always seemed tense and emotional these last few months because of the hardships we endured. The crooked nose you see me with today is a souvenir of Viet Nam.

Things were escalating and the overall morale was very low to the point some were considering re-upping, which meant one could go home, get another MOS (Military Occupational Specialty) as long as they extended two more years of military. About four soldiers from our company left weeks earlier to get out of harm's way. One soldier nicknamed "Red" asked me and a friend of mine for some advice as to whether or not he should re-up and go home. He said he had a feeling that he was going to be killed soon and felt his number was up and thought this would be the remedy to that. We discouraged him and said, "Red, you put eight months in already, you can make it another four." I regret giving Red that advice. During my time in the hospital with the scorpion bite the news came back Red had been shot in the back and died immediately on the scene. That really hurt! We couldn't get his face or his red hair out of our minds. I can still see his face. Imagine the emotional low when still another young man named Ed, only eighteen years old, who had been in country for only two weeks, also had been killed that day. After five and a half months and beginning with around 157 people in Charlie Company, due to injuries, deaths, and ended tours we were now down to 32. The decision came down from higher up that we were going to have to merge with Alpha Company. I was about to get one of the biggest breaks in my life. I was going to get out of infantry field duties and be sent to Da Nang. Now, at the end of this most intense battlefield period I was about to have all the questions I had been asking thus far answered and satisfied. *

CHAPTER 16

"OUT OF HARM'S WAY"

At this point my journey was about to change gears. I had been traveling at a high rate of speed emotionally. Just before I might have crashed, I was rescued and pulled out of the heavy traffic into a more tolerable speed limit. You've heard it said, "It's not what you know, but <u>who</u> you know." Auspiciously, I unexpectedly ran into a friend I had met during my college days, named Mark Johnson, who also had been serving at this same time in Chu Lai. We had a chance to talk about the good ole' days and everything going on during our tours. Mark had a desk job and after hearing about my combat blues, said he would talk to his captain about helping me to get out of the field. In his company there was going to be position opening to replace the current Army liaison, who was scheduled to go home soon. It was the choice between—a desk job or a grunt job! Not a tough decision for me. During my job interview with Mark's captain, I was asked if I knew how to type. I said, "Sure, of course, I was a college graduate just like Mark." The truth was, I didn't even know where the letter "A" was on a typewriter but for that job I was going to learn, quick! All the paperwork was made ready and my infantry captain, who was on his way home, then approved my new orders. This proved to be divine timing through a very small window of opportunity. I not only knew Mark Johnson but I also knew the One who created him. Mark was used by God to take me out of harm's way. This was to be the end to my combat duties and initiated my healing process. Thanks Mark, your consideration saved me so much misery. You were an instrumental player in my destiny.

Things instantly started to improve. I was headed for Da Nang, about eighty miles away, to serve as the Army liaison at the Air Force Base to the 22nd ASF (Aero-Medical Staging Flight). I was the only Army person on the airbase. That meant no bosses close-by. I had it easy from that point on compared to the rigors of infantry life. At times I had thoughts of guilt leaving those few behind in Chu Lai, however, those thoughts were fleeting and soon I never looked back. I was on another trek now, to a new environment with new people, strongly determined to make it home one day. I took with me, written on my heart, the faces, the friends and the memories of those past five and a half months, which seemed to last another lifetime.

Now what is this? Flush toilets? Would this mean I no longer had to use my adjustable entrenching tool to lean on while I did my business? Ice, could it be? Does this mean I will no longer have to roll my sodas on a block of ice, the former infantry tradition called, "rolling your own"? One thing after another was I finding on the Air Base, having an exclusively different ambience than Army life. The Air Force had their act together in Viet Nam. I had my own single bunk, a small fan that I bought for 10 dollars, which lasted until I sold it nine months later for ten, and I could turn it on full blast right in my face at night. There was a wash room with hot running water with SHOWERS! Now, this was more like it! I could make it here with ease. Did I fail to mention that there was a real movie theatre on base, a NCO club, and a cafeteria where you could eat hot meals and all you wanted plus breakfast served at midnight? I had joined the wrong branch of the service! It wasn't Club Med but for me it was in this war as far as I was concerned. I know I didn't deserve to have it this well or better than anyone else but thanks to all the prayers coming my way, I gratefully embraced it. I believe it was the favor of God!

My job consisted of each day talking to all the Army personnel who had been injured in warfare, airvacked to this hospital, treated and prepared to go back home to the U.S.A. I would interview each soldier to see whether all their personal belongings and records were in order and made sure those things were sent back to their next destination or home if necessary. It was a definite advantage for me to have had combat experience when it came to their cooperation and our communication. The responsibility for the official roster and record of each Army soldier that came here was mine and so I mailed that information back to Chu Lai to the Administration Building where Mark worked. That was the extent of my typing duties also. My "hunt and peck" typing technique became quite adequate for the task. That's why I can type this book today, Army training. I did a few other things to help the hospital staff when needed but overall my job was for the most part was the best in town. The doctors and nurses were the real heroes here. They unselfishly and competently worked around the clock trying to save lives and had a heart and compassion for everyone in their care. Their trauma from the continual visual display of wounded soldier casualties of war was more than you could fathom.

In the first bay were all the amputees. This was the toughest part of my job here. Day after day I had to speak to and see fellow soldiers who lost a leg, both legs, an arm, both arms, or all of the above. Some of the worst cases never made it out of here but were later taken to the morgue. One man had lost every limb and both his eyes to a land mine blast but somehow was still breathing. I always pondered, "Why bother living, this man has the worst of futures should he even make it." The people serving the wounded were a special breed of human beings. They truly cared every day for each patient and were determined to do their best to make them as comfortable as possible. This was someone's son, someone's brother, someone's dad or someone's husband. I felt so bad for those wounded. The first bay amputees for the most part shared a good attitude. The patients were surrounded on all sides by those in the same or worse condition. For one brief week they all had their afflictions in common. We would often comment, "I wonder what it is going to be like when the realization hits them back home, when there is no one except themselves without legs and they have to face the rest of their days this way?" Many do not live long, so I was told, because of complex circulation problems and some didn't make it home at all. Dear God! The ignominy of war! Flesh and blood killing one another day after day! A disgrace of creation! Ultimate corruption! *

CHAPTER 17

MY EPIPHANY

Months have gone by now and I've met some new friends. Seemed the majority here also smokes marijuana, including doctors, nurses, those enlisted and commissioned officers. That shocked me a little since I never had even the desire to smoke it, if you can remember back to the chapter on drugs where I ate the opium-laced cake. Dumb! It really didn't bother me if others used drugs, even those like Bill Clinton who said they only took a puff once but didn't inhale. I figured they had their own reasons and it was no business of mine. Readers, let's get real! We are living in a world that often times is a tragic "comedy of errors" whether you will admit it or chose to live in denial and feign ignorance. Most of my acquaintances occasionally got high to simply numb the reality of war's consequences they had witnessed. It was impossible to remove the faces of hurting people out of your consciousness.

Alcohol and drugs were popular escapes to dull one's senses. Music also had the power to change the atmosphere and allow one's departure into another serene realm. The music of the Beatles, the Temptations, Mo-Town, "Woodstock" and the like offered suitable backgrounds for both individual and group retreat. Conversations and philosophies continued nightly, though at times they were drug or alcohol influenced.

Some of us gathered together one day as usual to chat and the discussion turned to the subject of "Is there a God? And if there is, Who is He?" In the group were a couple of believers, some non-believers, including an agnostic and an atheist. I said, "Let's make a bet. If God exists, I win and if He doesn't, you win." So, I tried to explain to the atheist in a "Pascal's Wager" manner why I believe God exists and is real and **only** those who believe He exists will eternally be with Him in His Kingdom and I was willing to bet my life on it. The atheist wisely reasoned after hearing my beliefs, "You have nothing to lose if He's not real except this bet yet everything to gain, if He is. On the other hand, I have nothing to win if He doesn't exist but this bet, but possibly everything to lose including eternal life and this bet, if He does." I couldn't have scripted it closer to Pascal's Theory (Pascal was a French philosopher, 1623—1662). Finally, the consensus was, "God does exist, but the next question was, Who is He?" Many different answers surfaced, most of which were not consensual. So, once again as in many nights before, we again went to bed with that question unanswered. "God reveal to us who you are!"

We all did share one common sentiment, fear. After asking these questions and always searching for the answers to soothe our fears, at least temporarily, something amazing and life changing was about to take place. It was somewhere between two and three o'clock in the morning, when suddenly while I was asleep and the night was pitch black, I was awakened by an audible voice, an actual sound. It was an authoritative masculine voice, one that not only awakened me from a sound sleep, but also unnerved me. At the sound of this voice I began shaking as it emphatically said, "I AM LOVE!" The words were crystal clear, as if someone was standing over me with a microphone and speaking right into my ear. I looked around to see who it was that spoke these words to me. There was no one there. Perhaps it came from a radio. But it was two in the morning and everyone was sleeping. I thought, "maybe I was just dreaming." Now sitting up in bed, I thought I might just as well go back to sleep, when the same voice again repeated those same words, "I Am love!" This time I was awake for sure. My entire body started to shake from the vibration of that sound and even tremble. An unfamiliar, strange yet friendly heat filled my body from head to toe, whereby even the hair on my arms stood up. I knew in my heart of hearts that those words came from none other than God

Himself. That sound was the healing frequency of heaven! The reason I immediately knew that it was God was because of the release of the peace and warmth that totally permeated my being. The word "LOVE" then expanded and expanded to an illuminated understanding of everything and every query I had been searching for in my daily questioning. For me this was a miraculous event. Supernatural! God, Himself, had revealed to **ME** in a very real way His bottom line identity, Who He was, **LOVE**!

So, my very next exuberant thought was to go and tell somebody. So I went to tell my closest friend, who was also a believer, what had just happened to me. As I was walking to where he was supposed to be sleeping, I found it peculiar that he was on his feet heading towards me. When we were about fifteen feet away from each other, we both simultaneously pointed our index finger at each other and at the exact same time we said to each other, "GOD IS LOVE!" He said, "God just spoke to me." I said, "God just spoke to me too!" He spoke the same thing to both of us. This was the confirmation that this wasn't something imaginative, but real! We hugged each other while dancing around in a circle with joy. Others, now awake from our noise hollered, "Hey, Keep the noise down, we're trying to sleep. What's wrong with you guys, anyway? Do you know what time it is? Have you guys been smoking pot, or what?" No, we were not drunk as they supposed, just supernaturally high on God.

The Great "I AM", who had been with me throughout this war journey, revealed Himself as Love. I sensed this had been a set-up all along. Love became my entire theology. I heard His voice, felt His presence and received His Love. I found out later in a Bible verse, "that Perfect Love casts out fear." That's Who He is and that's what happened. The fear of death packed its bags and left my heart. What had taken place was that I finally opened the door of my heart and welcomed the King to enter so that the spirits of fear and death had to leave. I wish I had experienced that reality earlier in my life but today marked a new beginning. This was my epiphany! Of course I later found out this Christian principle: When anyone asks Jesus to become Lord of his life and then invites Him to enter the door of his heart and truly believes He shed His blood, died, and was buried and then resurrected to wash all sins away, the King will reside in you and protect you from all fear. This was the first step that triggered what would one day eventually become my full recovery. With that step and that event I had spiritually and emotionally transcended the environment of this world of cold reality of war and fear and had "crossed over" the threshold of the door into the Kingdom of God where I felt the presence of the King. However, my next dilemma would be—"How was I going to express and share all of this new found internal change?" *

CHAPTER 18

LETTERS SENT HOME

Have you ever been in a bad car accident? Can you remember when it first dawned on you that you were going to collide and how you seemed to enter into slow-motion and before you could move out of the way, crash! Can you still feel the dulling impact of that collision? How about the degree of shock you were not then fully aware of that you went into immediately following the whole incident? Wasn't it a bit bizarre how you first behaved and handled yourself? And further, did you ever try to explain that whole experience to someone who never had been in an accident? How tough was that? Better yet, have any of you ever had a full-grown pink elephant, while pole-vaulting, land on you while you were sunbathing? Of course you haven't! But suppose you had this happen to you and then you had to fully explain the details of this trauma to everybody. Where does one start? You would find out real soon no one could relate to your "recently squashed by an elephant" story. Well that is very similar to what I felt when I had to try to represent and communicate my war experience upon each occasion of mailing letters back home to my family and friends.

The toughest period I encountered during my letter writing was immediately after my "epiphany." I would mindfully try to illustrate in each letter my heart felt reenactment of the whole "God is Love" experience. Then I further attempted to delineate how that revelation of Love has clarified the entire purpose for my existence. Of course I wrote it with a new enthusiasm, total sincerity, and total passion! "All of creation was portrayed in Love, I wrote. Animals were put on earth for us because of His Love. Blue skies, green trees and clear running waters and the spectrum of all nature's colors are here for us to enjoy because God knew we would like the ones He picked out. This life is all about Love and God is Love!" I explained to everyone that fear no longer had any hold of me because it was overcome by God's Love. I continued by saying that I was going to live and not die because God Himself is protecting me and has spoken to me! That last statement lost my family audience, of course. To me it seemed to sound a whole lot better when I wrote all of that in the midst of my excitement than now as I'm writing this to you. Oh, don't get me wrong, I'm still excited to date but I'll bet some of you had the same response as my family members and friends who carefully perused these strange letters back then. Hope I didn't lose you like I did my family members and friends. I know this isn't a typical Hollywood theme.

They wrote back to me things like, "Well, that's real nice! Are you sure you are O.K.? Tell me, have you been taking drugs? Is the weather still about the same?" Yes, I'm O.K. No, I'm not taking drugs and the weather was still the same, hot, followed by hotter, and then "damn it's hot." They really didn't know what to think or reply either. How could they, unless they were there too? The consensus concluded that I was simply just "shell shocked" and must be suffering from "combat fatigue." That might have been a good assessment borrowed from World War II, and probably the best description they could muster. They just couldn't wrap their minds around my attempt to describe that elephant falling on me. It wasn't real to them! It was only real to me. Most people never have lived in ultimate reality, just their perception of it!

The truth is my communication with the home front from that point on was superficial because we were no longer connecting on the same plane of understanding. I was becoming more and more alienated from home and I could feel myself drifting ever so slowly away. The need to be understood was increasing but now the only ones who understood me were the ones with which I now shared my life still ten thousand miles away from home. The emotional departure from my loved ones was gradual and a source of periodic sadness. The only closeness we now shared was in prayer. I knew they were "for" me but they also felt the inability to change the given dynamics of being separated. Alienation had set its roots in place as evidenced by our diminishing letter exchange and their dwindling contents.

Now I had come to the point in this emotional marathon where I had to survive the rest of my obstacle course without considering them. Now it was just God and I, plus my few friends. Time was purposefully dragging its sluggish hands. Father Time would move five paces forward and then ten backwards. Have you ever had to spend a week alone away from your family? Day by day the distance seems more intolerable as the week goes by. How about trying a whole month? Now, try it for six months, being away from the people, who for the last twenty one years, you held so valuable. It seemed to be another lifetime! Now it felt surreal, like a bad dream at the point of frustration, a seeming fantasy world yet true reality. The contrast between my past reality and my present reality was intoxicating. The mounting pressure for some kind of change to take place soon in order to be removed from the total absurdity of this war was becoming more and more paramount. I needed a break from this humdrum and sterile environment. Well, Uncle Sam came to my rescue. He sent vacation papers for me to spend a week of rest and relaxation (R&R) in the island paradise of Hawaii! Thanks to my Uncle and all you taxpayers, I accepted the government's offer. I wrote to my wife and in time all the arrangements were made for us to meet in Hawaii. Maybe she would understand the "new changed me" and perhaps I would be able to at least communicate these deep feelings and the thoughts that I needed to express and be understood to confirm this new identity. She was leaving from Denver, I was leaving from Da Nang and we were rendezvousing in Oahu. This is just what the doctor ordered. It was going to be great, so I thought.

CHAPTER 19

REST & RELAXATION?

Don Ho! Tiny Bubbles! Night Clubs! Exotic food, drinking, dancing, music! Engleburt Humperdink! Polynesian women! Ocean waves and palm trees! King-size bed and room service! This was going to be an exciting meeting with my wife in Hawaii and my expectations were at an all time high. I was sure she was going to be as thrilled to see me as I was to see her. The beautiful ambience of the Hawaiian Islands was going to be a holiday in itself. What could be more romantic than that?

But whom was I kidding? Had I forgotten our rocky first year of marriage? We were trying to hold on to a relationship that from the beginning had its communication problems. Of course I was the biggest problem factor when put under the magnifying glass. I was not the leader, the husband, or the father I should have been. The reason was obvious; At 22 I was still selfish and immature at the time. I didn't then know the love of God and therefore I couldn't love others as He loved me nor communicate that. I practiced filial (brotherly) love with people some of the time and erotic (Eros) love with women some of the time but the unconditional, unselfish agape Love of God, I knew not how to apply. The bottom line of my idea of romance was mostly about loving myself and sex. It was still about me, not about loving God, not about loving others.

At one point in my marital relationship I actually welcomed my draft papers. They meant I would get away from my daily marriage responsibilities. The last time I was with my wife was during military leave before going to Viet Nam. At the same time my daughter, Cheryl, was having her first birthday. She was the cutest little girl, curly blonde hair and blue eyes and was then blowing out just one candle on her very first birthday cake. Because of school and work, I had very little bonding time with her before leaving to the service and now it has been more than six months once again that her daddy had not been there for her. Meanwhile my wife was now more than six months pregnant with our second child, who was conceived during the military leave that I mentioned.

Concentrating on my hardships in Southeast Asia, I often failed to consider the hardships my wife was also facing at her job, being pregnant, taking care of Cheryl by herself in my absence and having to live in the basement of my parent's house.

Unaware and ignorant of the true depth of each other's burden and pain from the past six months, we were about to meet head on and collide, each bringing along his own list of emotional baggage that would taint the meeting.

Do I need to tell you how awkward it was when we finally converged? We acted as if it were our first date. From the outside we each looked like the person we left behind but there had been a dramatic change taken place on the inside of each of us. We were both wounded. No matter what we said, it just didn't help us connect. We were strangers! The entire time we spent together seemed superficial, just going through the motions trying to have fun. We couldn't find the mechanism to release the emotional weight we carried. It was no one's fault.

Feeling alienated from her that first night together I even left the hotel room while she slept and visited a nearby nightclub. That was how the next days went with little improvement. We both tried to communicate and connect but nevertheless, other than changing the scenery, we failed to improve our circumstance. We soon said our goodbyes, wished the other the best and once again parted to catch the flights back to our separate lives. War can be the last straw that will strain or even break any relationship that was already fractured or had its shortcomings. Where do I go from this point?

It was a welcomed temporary escape but now it was time to go back to the world where again

I must turn on my automatic survival mode, but right now I'm not even convinced why. I've lost some of the motivation to return home after my latest marriage encounter. There seemed to have been a metamorphosis in process within me. The individual I used to be, that first came to Viet Nam, had somehow been altered by the exposure to cold reality to the extent that I felt I was undergoing a severe change in identity. By trying to toughen up on the inside in order to bear the encumbrance of this reality I was becoming emotionally hardened. I could also feel that being exposed to this ever-present darkness had taken its toll on me. Adversity will test character and my character was losing the battle. The ubiquitous abundance of lawlessness continually contaminated my thought life. Even though I knew better, yet since I had no further source for spiritual infilling in my life, I was becoming instead a victim of war's ugly influence and infilling. I was not cherishing the love revelation I had received because I couldn't seem to practically apply it. I didn't like the person I was becoming nor could I stop that process from happening. I had to put the revelation on hold for another day, a day when someone would finally understand and communicate with the new me. This would mark the end of the first half of my tour. I hope the next half is not going to be quite as confusing and chaotic! *

CHAPTER 20

A LETTER FROM MY BROTHER

Returning to the land of rice paddies, water buffaloes, poverty and oppression was a far cry from the temporary visual and material comforts of Hawaii. Of course a second thought entered my mind: Why not go and buy another airfare ticket headed to America or even Mexico? That wouldn't be a good idea in the long term, so I reluctantly yielded to my orders to return to duty.

Even the smell of the familiar air and the unfriendly heat and humidity reminded me I was back. There was nothing I could do but try to get settled back into the daily routine as soon as I was able and try to forget the "other" world out there. In case you had forgotten, it was so damn hot here inside the base with concrete and asphalt everywhere intensifying the heat. I was thankful at times when the weather dropped down to just "very hot." The external environment mixed with my internal environment sometimes made it almost unbearable.

War's internal victimization and emotional damage had been stored in the vaults of my heart's memory bank. I've become a new person. Proverbs 23:7 says,

> "As a man thinketh in his heart, so is he."

This simply meant I had become what I was now thinking subconsciously from my heart. Bottom line, I now have a heart problem, but not only did I not know what to do about it but also didn't even know what or that it was there. All the things I had been exposed to were so much in contrast with my former life in "Mayberry RFD" in the USA that it had turned my belief system and life paradigm upside down and inside out. I knew the sum total of these things I had experienced were real and so now my overall sense of reality had been expanded to include them. The events and scenes of the death and horror of war played over and over in my thoughts like a second rate "B" movie film.

They say your true character is who you are when no one is looking. Well no one was looking and for that I'm glad. Also it has been said that adversity builds character. That is of course, if you respond honorably to it. My character was struggling and lacking in immaturity. What would happen to you when you have no one to answer to except yourself and God, that is, if you even believe in God? War will bring out in you what you are really made of both good and bad. If you have been living your life in obedience to the rules only because there were penalties you feared for disobedience, what if all those restrictions were removed? Freedom without responsibility always ends in lawlessness, which promotes chaos and confusion. Can those of you having been involved in war to some capacity understand and relate to this scenario? Few people I knew back then rose up above the circumstances and weathered the storm. I proved I was no exception.

In about my eight month I received a letter from home. It came from my younger brother. He had also been drafted and was serving in the Army back in the states during his AIT period. Currently the military draft rule stated that brothers no longer had to serve in Viet Nam at the same time if they did not want to. Timing is everything. He was scheduled to go to Viet Nam at about the time I would have already left. He wrote and asked me if I would consider extending my tour so that he would have his orders changed so he could go elsewhere. As I sat down in the still of the night at my bunk, the thought of him having to experience the hell I had tasted deeply troubled me. There's no way I would want my brother to have to confront this absurdity and possibly lose his life over it. After all I was his big brother and needed to somehow help him remedy this situation. I loved him dearly, especially now after my epiphany and still do even though it has been many years since that letter had arrived.

To complicate this matter, the Army was going to send me home in just a couple of months for an "early out" or shortened tour. If I stayed here for a total of fourteen months, I could finish my total military obligation. After considering all the ramifications of my decision to extend my tour the choice wasn't difficult. I was reasonably safe here and who knew where they might send my brother. Besides, I felt very safe with God's right hand over me. I made up my mind; I was going to extend to fourteen months. As I was returning the letter that night in candlelight, I knew it would insure my brother's safety from the perils of Viet Nam. The end result was that his orders were going to be changed and he would now spend his tour in Seoul, Korea. He and his family were very grateful. It felt real good on the inside this time for being able to help him and put love into practice and know his family would then have some peace.

On a hot muggy, star-studded night and only a couple of weeks after I had sent that letter, the Da Nang Airbase withstood a rocket attack. One rocket hit a barracks just 100 feet away from us and lit up the entire sky while we were standing outside near the wall of another building! It blew that building up into the air and sent boards and wood splinters all over the place. It hit with the force and random devastation of a tornado with evil intentions. A rocket attack first announces itself by a hideous whistling noise followed by a thunderous crack and collision upon impact, much like lightning followed by thunder. Believe me it gets your immediate attention. The impact alone shakes every ounce of your being and body and leaves you with such a feeling of defenselessness and humility. There is nowhere to hide. We were all shook up for the next half-hour but had been spared. I knew that was how the enemy felt every time he was hit by our planes and artillery. At dawn we surveyed the damage the rockets caused. It was astonishing to find only a few buildings were hit. The remaining rockets missed their targets and no one was killed. During the attack I must admit that during the rocket attack the thought of my decision to extend my tour was in question for that brief moment. The hysterical impact of the attack had subsided, everything soon thereafter settled down and from that time forward I never again regretted my response or resolve regarding my brother's letter. *

CHAPTER 21

NOW, SIX MORE MONTHS TO GO

Man really is a resilient species. Given time he usually can adapt to just about any set of circumstances. That is where I have found myself rebounding from the combat experience, to the strain in my marriage relationship, to the decision to extend and now bouncing back with my overall attitude remaining positive and flexible for the final six months of this out-of-doors picnic. With all of this going on I still retained a smile and didn't loose my sense of humor, although now admittedly sometimes it was difficult. Now I'm trying to look at things in a more optimistic light. Not everything here was negative. There were good people going through the same experiences I was and doing the best they could. Friendships were paramount to one's well being. We all had a common denominator, "Let's do our time and get out of here as soon as possible." I shared my time and thoughts with a circle of friends and they made my life bearable. Overall they had a healthier attitude than I, because they had been spared from combat duty. Everyone who spent time in a war will come back with a unique and different story depending upon his overall perception, character make-up and the reception of the cards he was dealt.

One of my favorite times overseas was when I would hitch a ride to the South China Beach. After my work was finished in the morning I would go with some friends in the afternoon to the ocean to hang out. Not many people knew that there are beautiful places and sites in Viet Nam. Coming out of the jungle and now to a beautiful oceanfront was such a dramatic contrast. The geography and topography of Viet Nam are diverse. You can see triple canopy jungle with an assortment of animals, to sandy deserts with nothing but blowing wind, lizards and snakes, to miles of rice paddies and farm ground with villages, people and farm animals, to cities with buildings, automobiles, motor scooters, open air displays of fresh produce and meat markets. There were waterfalls, clear water rivers, mountains, ever present Coca-Cola vendors, banana popsicles delivered by the children to the field troops, and even beautiful waves at China Beach that I did take advantage of whenever possible.

Sometimes I would spend hours just looking out into the mysterious sea. Waves fascinate me to this day. I love the movement of the sea, its smell, its accompanying fresh gentle breezes and overall synchronized symphony of sounds, rhythm and tempo. Its overall power, like a gigantic muscle when agitated or at calm, I much respected. It features a spirit of recreation and amusement, a spirit of solitude and self-reflection, a spirit of freedom and life, even a spirit of fear and fatality for those unprepared. It also is a great playground for the world famous "Frisbee." We spent endless hours of entertainment with the illimitable application of the "art of throwing and catching" the Frisbee. I had friends who were considering changing their religions and becoming "Frisbyterians." Frisbyterians believed that when you died after years of faithfully throwing and catching the immortal Frisbee, one day your soul would simply fly upon a high rooftop where you could not get it down. See, I told you I didn't lose my sense of humor. We became frisbeeholics and at the same time were getting a great sun tan to go back home with. We learned how to body surf there and that was a blast! It was fun but at the same time once in a while you crashed! To this very day one of my favorite things is to walk along the sea with my wife, looking for sea shells, swimming, then sitting on lounge chairs, oiling up the skin, having a tropical drink, staring out at the sea while "catching rays" and breathing in the ocean breeze.

We would come back to work that night fully exhausted but totally refreshed. It was a kick. Times like this helped to forget the yesterdays. After work we went to the weight room around ten or eleven and lifted weights for exercise. I was blessed with strength and really built up my body during the process. After lifting we would walk to the mess hall and have a midnight breakfast. It included a custom made omelet of your choice of ingredients, pancakes or waffles, ham, bacon, or sausage, cold milk or juice, grits or hash browns to list a few. We had it made! Air Force food was tops! It was very enjoyable especially after a tough day at the beach. Oh yes, don't forget the movie theatre we had to attend weekly. Someone had to fill the empty seats and we felt it was our duty to do just that. These were the times that softened the stay and made it tolerable. I'm not trying to shove my good times in any soldier's face that never got the breaks I did. I'm just boasting about how blessed I felt by the favor of God providing this. What a stark contrast to the battlefield! Finally, I had become well adjusted to the heat, the environment, the job, the people and the recreation. Now it was just a matter of spending the remaining time day by day until I was free from this place and then ultimately free from military life. However, I do admire those who, on the other hand, enjoy this life and are called to be soldiers. My story isn't even close to those soldiers who had more horrific episodes during their combat experience. Nevertheless, one deeper, always pending problem that had not yet been dealt with for lack of knowledge was my heart problem that kept me from being totally free. *

CHAPTER 22

PART TIME FRIENDSHIPS, FULL TIME MEMORIES

From minutes to hours into days which became weeks that sluggishly added up to months until I was now considered a "short timer." Thanks to the daily routine and the law of diminishing returns, my time was finally coming to an end. That dark world where I seemed to be lost in a labyrinth, in an endless maze without an exit, was actually close to its conclusion. There was light at the end of the tunnel and it wasn't just another train. I wish I could describe my feeling just before departure. I never experienced getting out of prison but as far as I was concerned, leaving this country was as great as the mass exodus of the children of Israel from Egypt who were freed from bondage and the tyranny of the Pharaoh.

Jerome Arnold, nicknamed "Big," an Air Force E-4, became my best friend during my term at the 22nd ASF. We got along better than brothers. We often talked about our dysfunctional lives in the past, the things we liked back home and our future life returning to the "real world." I learned a lot about the black man and he likewise learned about the white man. He showed me how to tie a double knot on a necktie and dress up. I taught him how to lift weights and body building. He introduced me to his culture and his favorite music and musicians, especially Mow Town and the "Temptations." I helped him train to be a football player and even wrote a letter of recommendation to Eddie Crowder, then the University of Colorado's head football coach, so that Jerome would be considered for an athletic scholarship when he left Viet Nam. We shared fun, trouble, laughter, work, meals, and each one's perception of the overall war experience, all to make the clock more tolerable. Staff Sergeant Walters, a friend of ours and a Marvin Hagler look alike, was the "badest dude" I had yet to meet. He had been a student of the martial arts and one day told me to call the Military Police in five minutes and call an ambulance. I asked, "Why?" Jerome told me, "Never mind, just do what he said!" Walters entered the NCO club as Jerome and I went to call the MP's. Jerome explained to me a couple of guys called Walters a "nigger" and he felt it was his duty to teach them some communicative manners. As we returned to the NCO club after phoning, we saw the military police arrive to find two guys knocked out and propped up against the NCO club's wall. They asked us if we saw what happened and we replied, "No!" We didn't lie. We knew what happened but we didn't see it. Walters joined us later and took us in a jeep with a ROK (Republic of Korea) marine into downtown Da Nang (Off limits) to celebrate his first round knockout of the overmatched tag team. Did I mention we were up to no good in Da Nang? You can use your imagination to reveal the goings on that evening! I told you lawlessness was the norm in wartime.

I'd like to thank my roomy Ken Stogner from Louisiana, also an Air Force E-4, who readily tolerated my presence. I wrote to him after he left country but I hadn't made contact with him since. Ken and Jerome and a couple of other friends hooked me up with an assortment of casual clothing so I could would be well dressed as I was about to take another R&R in Hong Kong, China. You get one R&R every six months. Jerome saw to it that I had plenty of spending money but please do not ask me how he arranged for me to get it. This time I was going to go with some friends who were determined to celebrate a week of freedom in an ever-rowdy manner. Hong Kong was a most interesting place to visit. It was filled with more than four million people and places, such as the Great Wall, that added adventure and intrigue to the experience. I won't tell you how many hookers and bars that filled every street and street corner you traveled. Crowded place! People and laundry were hanging out of the windows of multitudes of high rises which had a unique variety of businesses and/or living quarters on every floor of these skyscrapers. It wasn't unusual for more than one entire family to be living in a one- room dwelling. The food was fresh, the scenes were diverse and unrivaled and the mischief was plentiful. A week in Hong Kong with a group of young soldiers has the makings of yet another book, R-rated.

All these remembrances and associations I was now about to take home with me as I was preparing to say goodbye. This life is all about the people we meet along life's journey, those we touch and those who touch us at each bus stop towards one's ultimate destiny. These people and many others helped carry me through the process. I hope their memory of Robert Scheck, the Army guy, carried a mutual fondness and enhanced time of encounter. I held the total of this in the memory department of my heart labeled "Part time friendships, full time memories" of my time in Viet Nam to be opened at a later date. I have only opened up the headlines for you. The details are still very vivid to me. I just don't go there!

Tears filled my eyes and love filled my heart as I hugged and said goodbye to my friends I had bonded with as we shared the difficult time together. It was a very tender, bittersweet moment, one I remember, knowing that I probably will never see any of these people again. We have made it through this phase of our personal war and now we were going to take it back home with us. I grabbed my small duffel bag, jumped in the jeep, like a member of the "M.A.S.H." TV crew and waived to all as I was headed to the airport to catch the "Freedom Bird" that would take me home. *

CHAPTER 23

THE "FREEDOM BIRD"

A MAJOR CONSIDERATION on every soldier's mind just before he arrives to his war destination is "How will I get out of here?" Well, that's simple! The same way you got there, only in the opposite direction. For 365 days, more or less, you dream of taking that flight back home. It became your ultimate goal. We had a name for this cherished materialization, the exodus flight of "The Freedom Bird." It represented our Savior and Noah's Ark all wrapped in one. It meant getting off the dismal merry-go-round and leaving the amusement park. It symbolized our liberation like the freedom of an eagle in flight, thus Freedom Bird! For me the myth of ever leaving this situation now became a reality as I proudly and jubilantly climbed aboard the 747 stretch jet. Silently enjoying each and every step of the stairway, I greeted the stewardesses with a smile of elation. My smile was from ear to ear as if the night before I had gone to bed with a coat hanger in my mouth. For a year we all had fantasized about seeing beautiful stewardesses on the plane ride home. Actually we just wanted to see any beautiful woman. Would you believe any woman? That unfortunately was not quite the case. The women were older, tired, and far from an amorous mood. God bless them! The US Army in its wisdom figured, if two hundred lonely GI's got on a 28-hour freedom flight with beautiful women, there could be a riotous insurrection motivated by sheer testosterone and a party out of control.

As the plane lifted off the ground, there was a deafening cheer accompanied by a unanimous applause from all aboard. We looked out the windows intently as the world below slowly diminished until there was no land in sight. An audible sigh of relief echoed throughout the company-sized aircraft. We were finally safe! It occurred to me there were as many unique individual stories on board as there were filled seats. Each person was bringing back his own exclusive heart video to the states. Some videos were more graphic than others. Some were more damaging than others. All returnees had one common denominator, they indeed had been there and had been exposed to humanity's ultimate negative environment and predicament.

Nowadays on the longer flights some of the airlines offer a newly released movie for the passengers. On our 28-hour flight there was no movie, so instead, from my heart's memory video, I played the reruns and highlights of the last fourteen months of an almost surreal existence. Familiar faces and events kept flashing by. The faces of those that would never make it home one by one passed by in review as if I was saluting each one from the depths of my heart and making my last personal tribute in recognition of their ultimate sacrifice. The faces of friends, soldiers, children, workers, U.S. allies and all the people that played a role in this drama, seemed to appear as in a parade so that they too would be included forever in the final credits following my movie. I didn't know what emotion to employ throughout the cavalcade of those countenances fresh on my mind. At times I felt joy mixed with sorrow, happiness with sadness, lonely yet not alone, relieved yet burdened, even somewhat melancholy knowing these faces representing real lives would soon be just a video slide of my past on the way to my future destiny. Even today as I write these words I sometimes wonder how their lives have turned out since that histrionic episode we all shared. Where have all the soldiers gone? What a worldwide library of stories!

During the flight I recalled the day when our company had to climb a heavily foliated hill in order to capture an enemy hospital complex that was hidden by triple canopy jungle. Rushing to the top of a hill is much like pushing a rope. Two-thirds the way up, considering the heat, the climb, my rucksack being 100 pounds, I had to stop and take a breather. This hill would have challenged Lance

Armstrong. By the time we finally took the hill, Charlie simply had run down the other side. It was oh so quiet as we carefully walked the grounds of the hospital complex so that you could have literally heard a pin drop. We looked for snipers even up in the trees as we slowly surveyed the area. Then, all of a sudden a loud voice spurted out, "F#*# You!" It seemed to come from nowhere. Then again, "F#*# You!" It was the sound made by the native "gecko", also called the insulting lizard. I was told earlier about this lizard but thought it was just the local joke for the new ones arriving to the camp, kind of like bagging "snipes." Only the people who have heard this lizard can attest to its off color "HBO" language. Imagine a Vietnamese lizard that could only speak this one word of English! Believe it or not, its outburst unnerved us. Capturing a hospital was like kissing your sister, not much victory. Thoughts like this came and quickly passed to another.

Event after event replayed in vivid detail perhaps as if I was attempting to bring final closure to the entire affair. There were so many things not fitting to remember or write about yet I have retained them by the sheer ability and recollection power given to man by God. Of course closure at this point was going to be impossible. Even though I tried, I had to admit I was so fully saturated with the freshness of my thoughts embracing the whole experience to finally realize that only with time will all of this be put behind me. It was time to forget once drinking black, smelly rice paddy water, which I swore I would never do unless I was dying of thirst and until at one point I was. It was now time to change my focus and try to turn off that video switch. It was time to take a break and put my introspection on the shelf for the time being.

My attention now shifted to my next destination, the good old USA. The feeling that I was really free was overwhelming. I caught myself grinning, now and then, the entire trip home. Thank you, Jesus, for providing for me and protecting me and delivering me home with all my body parts in tact! I was in a pleasant state of shock and yet unbelief. To think that one minute I was there and the next minute I was rescued and plucked out of the entire scene! A feeling of ecstasy! It was for me-rapture!

First stop was going to be Fort Lewis Washington, where within a couple of days I would be released from my military obligations in the US Army. That was the day I cherished and at times thought would never emerge. Now I will have faithfully served the country I love and absolutely appreciate even more, will have made the sacrifice every citizen owes the land he chooses to live in, and will undoubtedly be honored by all upon my return…or so I thought! *

CHAPTER 24

BACK HOME IN THE GOOD OLD USA

As soon as we deplaned, we immediately kissed the ground and were so very grateful to touch American soil once again. "Home sweet home," was the unanimous sentiment. The price one pays for freedom to breath the air, see the sky and touch the earth of your homeland, even though your very life is at stake, is invaluable, better said, priceless! The high cost of "freedom" is the essence of life itself. The Bible says,

> "Greater love has no one than this, than to lay down one's life for his friends."

That is what Jesus did for us. To know that I went to Viet Nam so that my family, my brother Roy, my friends and countrymen would not have to, gave me great consolation.

However, back then there was no ticker tape parade, no crowd at the airport cheering and applauding as if their favorite team had just returned from the championship game, no wife to hug and kiss, no military welcome whatsoever. There was just a familiar olive drab bus to take us to Fort Lewis to eventually ETS, the term for terminating your service obligation. No, there was not even a handshake, a pat on the back or a good meal, just a final paycheck in fifty-dollar bills that was held back until you trimmed your sideburns and got a haircut. Even though I hesitated a moment to do that, it was O.K. for me! A stack of fifties, a clean uniform to wear home, and a new beginning in the United States of America was more than enough. Anyway, in a few hours I wouldn't have to ever cut my hair again, I thought. Besides, my grandmother was going to meet me outside the base and take me by bus to her home.

I felt like a back woods country boy blindfolded and taken to see downtown New York City for the first time when the blindfold was removed. Tall buildings, modern cars, busses, American people dressed in suits, dresses and normal attire walking about, street noises, rush hour traffic, paved streets and sidewalks, were such a welcome sight! Home! Houses! Supermarkets! Drive-by fast food! Apple pie and baseball games! There were no more rice paddies, no more barbed wire, no more people dressed in black pajamas, no more mine fields, and no more military life ever again! What an immediate stark contrast to where I had been! I was markedly still in shock and couldn't wrap my mind around all of this at once. If there was actually a real "Twilight Zone" I felt I had just entered and now exited it.

This was going to be a special time for me with Grandma. She had always been a loving, giving woman and when we saw each other and embraced that day her hugs and kisses were all the family welcoming party I needed. Unfortunately, that short encounter was to be the last time that we would ever see each other again in this lifetime. The rest of the passengers on the bus just ignored me in my military uniform with all the medals and patches that screamed out, "He just got home from Viet Nam!" Was that the way it was going to be everywhere I went? Yes, as time proved it to be so. Unlike the heroes of the war today that returned with honor, those that came back from Viet Nam never experienced praise or esteem. That exact deprivation of gratitude needed for personal fulfillment to justify their sacrifice is a latent heart condition of many who still haven't yet fully healed today and have not filled that empty reserved space. This was compounded by the feeling we had lost a war that we couldn't win.

Now that I was free, the thoughts entered my mind, "Should I go straight home? Or, should I spend a little time of mischievous diversion and go see an old fling? Should I even return home at all?" All those temptation thoughts came at once, because over the course of my exposure to the lawlessness of war and combined with my already flawed character, my conscience and my morality had been further altered and damaged in making correct moral decisions. My character was fractured and darkness had taken its toll. Besides, I even had a little cash and a potential whole new life out in front of me. That struggle waged its own war in my consciousness. Do I choose right or wrong? Where does my revelation of love fit? I wanted to celebrate and just party! Right Now! The very fact that my destination decision took time and posed a choice with which I struggled pointed to a severe division within my new belief system. Considering and them reconsidering the cost, I eventually chose to go home, however, reluctantly. The reason for my reluctance was one day going to have to be dealt with. Even though I came back with the knowledge that "God is Love," my ability to put to practice that kind of love had not yet been mastered. By what or by whom or how was I going to become whole or sane or stable on the inside? I knew deep down I was divided against myself, teetering up and down, my moral plumb line was swaying back and forth as in a sea of confusion. Nothing anchored me. My heart had no consistent compass. Troubled but free, well, truthfully not fully free, I once again set my course and destiny on automatic survival mode and headed for the home I once knew as familiar. What I was about to emotionally confront next upon arriving at Stapleton Airport, in Denver, bordered on surreal. *

CHAPTER 25

MAJORING IN DIVERSION, MINORING IN ELATIONSHIP

Up to the time I was drafted into the service, my young life was filled with success upon success. Whether in school, in sports, in work or in play, I prospered. Awards and honors came often for the many achievements and accomplishments on the way. These things I really enjoyed both in education and recreation. The things I learned, those things I valued, the success in sports, were available in abundance. My life had been blessed and very simple until I entered into a new territory, a social science and communal technology, underdeveloped on my part, called relationship. Even though I grew up in a large family of eleven, at that time I had just a minor degree in that course of study. Like most, I learned by trial and error and never read a "how to" relationship manual to speak of. All along I wasn't aware that the original relationship manual was contained in the greatest book ever known to man, the Holy Bible, the very Word of God. I simply and unfortunately overlooked the fact that the Divine Manufacturer of Relationships, Himself, inspired the Bible, which contains the blueprint for truth and wisdom in relationship. My first, up close and personal relationship with a young woman and those thereafter reflected my ignorance of this matter. Each relationship I had with the opposite sex, therefore, never improved, which now takes me to the then current marriage relationship I had upon my arrival home to Denver, Colorado, where I was met by my wife and children.

The details from that first encounter with my wife and children up to and ending with the day I decided to leave home are still very sketchy. Maybe it was merely a case of convenient selective memory loss or the simple fact that at that time I was still in a state of numbness and in a fog. When combined with my lack of finesse in marital communication, it was almost as if I was suffering a hangover equivalent to a fourteen-month drinking binge accompanied with a 10,000-mile jet lag. It all happened and deteriorated so fast in a blur, like being "beamed up" from the future on Star Trek's "Enterprise" and then materializing on another planet in the past. I was going through the motions of looking alive and pretended to be happy and O.K. but really felt disconnected from the responsibilities and accountability of life's routine back home again in the "former world." While I peered out through the windows of my eyes at those I knew, they all appeared to be exactly the same as when I left. However, when they returned eye contact to me, there was someone on the inside of my skin somewhat different looking back at them. I felt the new me was hiding the changed person inside my earth suit and only impersonating the one they used to know. When I saw my youngest daughter for the first time, she too seemed so distant and unfamiliar. That wasn't fair to her! So, why did I have to feel this way? I know this sounds so strange, but this is the only way I know how to explain it. There simply was not enough time to transition or adjust and make compatible the two contrasting worlds I now embraced. I was divided against myself. Even though these people were not strangers, I felt like the alien.

While going through the motions of a married life the next few months, I fell back into something that had been familiar to military life, male bonding. I had spent so much time with my military friends and so little time with family that I once again sought that type of customary companionship. It took the form of softball, basketball and sports of any kind to replace what I had been accustomed to in the military. Playing games, competing, winning and celebrating with drinking afterwards offered me what I thought I needed to enjoy my new existence. This form of enjoyment became a wedge between my wife and me, because now that the activities with my friends were excessive, I spent a lot of time away from home and my family. I played more softball and basketball games than some professionals. It was a convenient excuse to be irresponsible and to get out of the house. Remember, my problem was that I still was looking for a new identity that was compatible with the person on the inside. With the drinking came the temptation to socialize with other women. The intrigue of meeting other women spiced up my otherwise dull life with illicit romance. The entire enjoyment scenario was simply a counterfeit life philosophy and faulty belief system that had me looking for love in all the wrong places. After all, wasn't the philosophy of the day, "Make love, not war?" I've tried war but now it was time to make love or what I thought was love. Do you sense the contradiction between the revelation I had, that God is Love, and the love I was pursuing? The bottom line was I really didn't practically know love at all. I found "Eros" love, the erotic, sensual kind of love through sexual promiscuity. It felt good temporarily but was never fulfilling and never was satisfied outside of the marriage relationship.

I certainly do not blame all the people back home, my family, my parents, brothers & sisters and friends for not understanding me, because I didn't have a handle on my new attempt at identity myself. Most people haven't a clue what to do when war requires an adjustment period to reunite and re-acclimate relationships. As I have stated before, if there was any trouble or a crack in the foundation before, now it will multiply and continue to fracture. I was on a one-way track and didn't know how to stop the train. Communication now had failed because I not only could no longer relate to my wife but also did not have the will to do so. It was as if the former restraints to do what a responsible person, father and husband should do had all but left me. The influence of the lawlessness I experienced in war now was overriding my moral sense of responsibility and I was in rebellion to both God and my own conscience. After several months of this pretense claiming, "I needed my space," (an over-used shallow, double-motivated excuse) I packed my car with some of my things, said goodbye to my wife and kids and went down the "highway of selfishness and confusion." My wife and daughters were the innocent victims of my malady. It was never the question about their personal worth and value. I couldn't care for them as they deserved while I needed some type of care myself with the time to heal and recover from my condition never before treated. The reason I couldn't feel love for them is because I had not fully realized that I had hardened that love department in my heart to survive the atrocities of war. I had turned off the heart switch to the touchy, feely, sensitive part of me. It hurt too bad inside to feel the pain of those soldiers who died from our company and even those of the enemy.

I'm not trying to say that all returnees will respond this way but most of the ones I knew had a similar experience upon coming home. Now that one has decided to turn away from his former responsibilities, he heads down the path of temptation. The minute one chooses to cross over the invisible line of darkness it might be a very long time before he comes to himself. Unfortunately some will never find their way back. While always feeling something is lacking and being emotionally deficient because of the need for love, most people are on the path to choose what they think will be a reasonable substitute to fill that void and lack, usually with a superficial replacement. For some it will be a rebound relationship with someone who has no clue how much emotional baggage you are carrying with you. For some it will be frequenting the local neighborhood bar, like "Cheers," an imitation church with its pastor, the bartender. Of course there will be a sort of fellowship with new friends and family, "where everyone knows your name," where you can even play a tune on the juke box if you need praise and worship music to celebrate and toast after downing a few glasses of the alcohol spirit. For others it might be the streets where you meet your new friends, who at first will give you drugs for free, but later free proves very costly and those friends prove not to be friends at all. Some will end up homeless after a series of losing one thing after another: their marriage, their children, their house, their job, their car, their health and finally their life. In case you haven't kept in touch with today's reality, this is actually what is happening and escalating with time in every city and every community right before our eyes.

Shouldn't there be some type of debriefing and adjustment period with education and ministry after war experience? There should be but there isn't a sufficient system yet in place. The Bible says in Hosea 4:6, "My people are destroyed for lack of knowledge." I made several weak pitiful attempts on my behalf to reconcile with my family. I left and lived with some friends having similar identity and unknown destiny problems. I would leave them and come back home only to leave once more. This cycle repeated over and over and soon I destroyed my first marriage and deeply wounded the hearts of the innocent victims of my ignorance, lawlessness and selfishness. I would even take my daughters to meet my girlfriends. One daughter upon returning to her mother declared, "Now, I have two mothers!" How sad it was to put them through my conflicts. I can't even totally blame the war on my condition but its influence greatly contributed in helping push me over the edge. Ultimately, I was the one to blame. There was a defect in my overall belief system and my heart was unstable. An invisible yet real new war was being waged on the inside of me that I couldn't wrap my mind around, however, there was One and only One, who once spoke to me and was still on the inside of me, who will one day put an end to my war.*

CHAPTER 26

WHERE IS LOVE?

YEAR AFTER YEAR went by and relationship after relationship did the same. I was looking ceaselessly for LOVE or that ever evasive illusion of its reasonable facsimile. I later remarried but carried the same loveless heart condition into that marriage. Why couldn't I get my life together? It seemed as if everything I tried to build eventually fell down and collapsed. I resembled a house with no foundation and a builder who lost the blueprints. My life was going around and around in circles on an endless merry-go-round ride very much like the children of Israel doing lap after lap around Mount Sinai for forty years. My destiny remained unclear and I was a man without purpose or direction. I was playing the lead role in my own movie video that had no ending or known script. I was searching for something or somebody to help stop this monotonous pattern but my heart's compass couldn't find north. "What a tragedy it was, I thought, to spend an entire lifetime always going nowhere but always succeeding ending up there." There had to be some method to this madness and some reasonable meaning to this journey called my life which had been drowning in a sea of futility.

My second marriage started with excitement. A brand new adventure! A new start! A second chance! I was determined not to make the same mistakes as before in my past marriage this time. The problem, however, was that my heart's turn on switch still could not find the LOVE frequency or the channel. My wife claimed time after time, "You just don't love me as much as I love you!" I couldn't argue that point. I merely replied, "This is all the love I have! Take it or leave it." She left it! After ten roller coaster years of emotional ups and downs during my 2nd marriage, the undesirable ending became inevitable. Since I was the designated driver and leader of this marriage odyssey but had no clear vision of where I was taking my wife and family, this marriage too resulted in its ill-fated conclusion. Because I didn't know where I was going to take them, I shouldn't have even asked them to get on the ride for the non-stopping circular spin. Another relational disaster! Another relationship failure! A vicious cycle ending in its familiar fashion! I found myself once again existing in "Nowheresville", steadily spiraling downwards to the city of "Idontcare" on the way to "Lonelytown" located in the apathetic state of "Justdontmatter."

For the next two years I slipped, I stumbled and I fell, once more looking for the true meaning of this short life. That might be too understated! Actually, the truth is, I crashed and hit rock bottom.

What will I do now! Divorced again! The cycle is repeating itself on its own power and I've burned up the brakes. A precedent that began back in Viet Nam, now has resurfaced. I'm reverting again to the world of chaos and confusion. I'm revisiting the world of loneliness and darkness. I had been there before and had done that before. I didn't think I could go even deeper into that lifestyle this time. Yet, I had and so I've returned to the bars, nightclubs and beer. Is that all there is? Here goes that familiar Peggy Lee song playing on my heart's juke box, "Is that all there is, and if that's all there is, let's break out the booze and have a ball, if that's all there is!" I know some of you have been there! Being needy! Love, "Where are you?" LOVE! "I'm searching for you!" However, the law of diminishing returns had already been activated many years before. What I was looking for could not be found externally in the bars or answered by the companionship of a woman. Is there any future hope for me, not to mention what has happened to the kids, the innocent victims? What has happened to my wife? I didn't even have time to consider their plights. I was too wrapped up in my own whirlwind of self-pity. Where do I go from here? The Bible says, "A dog returns to his vomit!" That didn't sound like a great option or meal.

Everything I didn't like to do and everything I didn't want to be was happening all over again. Even take notice please of that which I have written with the above verbs: such as-<u>re</u>visiting, <u>re</u>verting, <u>re</u>turning-all with the same prefix, <u>re</u>-, meaning again! History is repeating itself and stuck on the stupid mode. What I needed was <u>re</u>-demption, <u>re</u>-conciliation, <u>re</u>-storation and possibly a re-birth!

Love had been waiting all along patiently on the inside of me this entire time just waiting for permission to answer all the questions of my dilemma. Love had never left me, had never abandoned me but had been in the offing for me to recognize and acknowledge its presence ever since it was first announced audibly back in Viet Nam.*

CHAPTER 27

COMING HOME FOR THE FIRST TIME

I HAD MERELY existed during the long two years after my divorce, when out of the blue I received a phone call from my second wife. She sounded pretty good on the phone and strangely enough rather much stronger than she had in the past. She caught my interest to the point that I eagerly continued listening to the advice she had for me. She said with authority, "Robert, what you need to do is to take two weeks off from going to the bars and take two weeks off away from your friends. Literally change your playground and playmates. Then try reading the gospel of John in its entirety. It is the gospel of Love. When you are finished reading it, give me a call." So reluctantly, and within a few days of my usual rebellious procrastination, I began to read the Bible according to John. I thought, "What do I have to lose, why not?" I was going nowhere fast at the time, anyway. So, I began to read John's gospel very slowly and often only one chapter at a time because I couldn't stay awake. There was something inside that didn't want to hear this gospel while on the other hand, surprisingly, something caused me to continue to read further that kept my interest. When I did finally finish reading the last chapter and verse, something amazingly emotional happened to me that very instant that I couldn't immediately explain. It was like fireworks going off in my understanding. Following that, I could only describe it as a peace enveloping me, a sobering blanket of tranquility, a complete ease that made me feel real GOOD and warm all over! I soon recognized that feeling! I had experienced this same thing once before in Viet Nam. It was the loving voice touch and presence of God that became alive by reading His Word. It was very familiar! I tasted it long ago and longed to return to that place, that moment, that peaceful reality and presence. For the first time in many years I had returned to the exact spot where I first met Peace in person. It felt like home sweet home had found me. Of course later I realized this environment was my original home. The very home atmosphere that mankind lost when he fell from the Garden of Eden. IT IS CALLED THE KINGDOM OF GOD, the kingdom that had been restored to earth by the loving sacrifice of Jesus Christ on the cross. I knew from within the King, Himself, had orchestrated my way back home. Through all the trials, the difficult events of my life's passage, war, divorces, drinking and promiscuity, accompanied with the many people who played a role in my finding my way home, it finally came down to again hearing the sound of the voice of my Master speaking to me one more time from the gospel of John. This gospel is spiritually alive and living with the power to bring any and all prodigals back home, all those who had been lost in darkness. I can not explain it any other way! Today I have realized the Spirit of God, who had never abandoned me throughout all my peaks and valleys, who was forgiving my sins, my shortcomings and the like, was the One who led me home! My heavenly Father welcomed me home to His spiritual kingdom here on earth just as it is in heaven. My story doesn't end here. This was only the beginning of my rehabilitation. It continued from blessing upon blessing to the point I had to write another entire book to tell you all the details. I can't wait for you to read my further success story in the book entitled "Unshakable Marriage." The book explains how my second marriage, after two years of divorce, was miraculously reconciled and that today my wife and I and our children are living happily ever after.

CHAPTER 28

MY FINAL THOUGHTS TO THOSE COMING BACK HOME FROM WAR

TODAY, LOOKING BACK over a generation in time, I would like to offer my wisdom and advice regarding this ever so imminent subject of those returning from Iraq, war, natural disasters, traumatic hospitalizations and the like. The person, the soldier, who returns to the places and people he left behind, will not be the same one that comes back. His heart has been dramatically changed. I would like to offer my understanding and categorize them on three levels:

> Category 1. The individuals, who were fulltime military, such as administration, clerical personnel, supply and troop support, who worked in a well protected

area called the "rear." These came back with little exposure to combat action and usually are going to be the least affected or stressed by their tours of duty. To a majority of them, it is business as usual. They will have to adjust to their family, however, by learning how to communicate again and shorten the relational distance they experienced while away until they become intimate once again. Please allow as much time as one needs for each family member to acclimate simply due to a year's absence. They will need some private quiet time to adjust for the all things they heard and felt regarding the part they played in a "war" environment.

Category 2. The individuals, who were involved indirectly with the trauma of the seriously wounded and/or had to deal with any phase of death or dead bodies, will need personal attention by qualified personnel. They are people such as doctors, nurses, medics, hospital personnel, emergency crews and the like. They dealt with the combat casualties and things of that sort. They will take much more time to readjust to their families, friends and selves. I believe they should have a structured plan and strategy for healing their thought life and emotional life. Some might need some spiritual counsel, depending on the degree to their exposure of the "war" and what they have seen up close.

I Never Came Home

Category 3. Finally, there are those individuals, who have been on the front lines of combat, infantrymen, specials forces, pilots, helicopter personnel, track units, and such who have faced live action combat and have seen death, and either have been seriously wounded or have been with seriously wounded comrades and will carry those pictures around in their heart's memories. These individuals could have faced the trauma to such a degree that they might have been dramatically changed to the point you will not recognize them and they will have difficulty in relating with you. They need to be held over and not let return home until they are assessed for internal damage by qualified personnel through valid testing. I also believe the family members should have to attend readjustment seminars for their understanding of the returnee. They will need the most time and counsel of all. Don't set a time limit on these. Each person will differ in what they personally need for recovery. Some will need physical therapy, some emotional therapy, and some need spiritual therapy as I had. Some might need all of the above. This type of trauma often so deep rooted it leaves emotional scars. It can not only be tough to identify but also for some a disorder never before properly diagnosed.

Of course these suggestions are not a science but just a skeletal example of the different depths of pain that requires healing. From the evolution of war terms such as battle fatigue to shell shocked to PTSD—Post Dramatic Stress Disorder you can see this condition intensifying as time moves forward. I'm pleased to see a detailed scientific study is being made by our government and many qualified private entities that will lend help in all the categories I simplified above. I would like to see no one left out that needs help even when they might not think so. This is a day when the Church needs to rise up and become trained in the ministry to help these mentioned. There will be of course exceptions to all rules. But please do something! Pray! Pray for them! Someone prayed for me and my entrance into the Kingdom. Don't be ignorant of so many relational difficulties they will face. Don't ignore them. This has become par for the day we are living in. It is more complicated today than in years past. Personal war has escalated. Substance abuse has reached a most bizarre level. Otherwise we will continue to have maladjusted, untreated, abandoned individuals infiltrating society and possible reeking havoc in every arena of this planet Earth. You will have to learn to communicate and relate, for the most part, anew. The new contents inside the earth suit he is wearing have been altered. The reality of the past he once knew has also been tainted. Most people have never lived in the ultimate reality of God's kingdom but instead have settled with their own opinionated perception of reality. Whichever being the case, those returning home and those receiving the returnees must allow time for healing and understanding that is necessary according to the extent of the trauma.

Man as a species is resilient, however, and because survival comes inherent by his very nature, he will endure. Each individual's scenario will vary as to his perception of reality and experience with trauma. Today's Ministry Leaders are aware that those returning and their families must be healed spirit, soul and body. You see, the wounds go deeper than the physical level, more extensive than the emotional gamut. They go down even to the depth of one's very spirit and subconscious mind.

The U. S. military, so far, has not been able to minister to the deep-seeded heart problems and needs of the veteran soldier and his extended family. How possibly could they? They need to interact with all the community with so many cases, too numerous, so complex and with the limited personnel and resources dedicated to this task? There are not enough psychologists, psychiatrists, mentors, case workers, specifically trained with the technology needed today in our ever so increasingly complicated world. If it takes a village to raise one child, it will take a national effort to heal them.

I'm trying to stress that you can help by your new understanding. They need space. They need time. They need help. They need love. All debriefing falls short. They need to be nursed back to health just as much as one that has been critically wounded physically or diseased. The only thing that helped me in the long journey home was to check into the heart doctor, Doctor Jesus, the one that created my heart. Your hope was and is my hope, Jesus Christ. He is Love and Love never fails! Love from all of you can save a life, a family and a future.

This is where the war must finally end. It is where all wars begin. This is where today the churches must rise up and learn how to minister to the entire three-part being, spirit, soul and body. Presidents, state and local leaders must one day have the personal revelation that there has always been a spiritual struggle between the kingdom of light and the kingdom of darkness. Everyone is a citizen and promoter of either one or the other. Without understanding the "Big Picture," we will continue to only treat topically the traumatic issues of life. We must turn to the Creator, the Savior, Jesus Christ, and the Helper, the Holy Spirit of God, for the solution to mankind's plight. Our greatest battles are from within before they ever externalize.

Please seek help from the sources who understand. Desensitizing one with drugs, booze, or withdrawal, never treat the real wound. Seek first the Lord, His Kingdom and His Word and those trained to help your loved ones. Pray daily, meditate on His Word, read the gospel of John. Use whatever means you have to reconnect with the "Healer" by faith, Who is ever willing to bring your loved one back home. I continue to pray for all of those who need this revelation for their own personal war to end. That is why I wrote this true story. At last I have become whole, and with the help of God you can have hope also for full, complete recovery. I sincerely love, honor and appreciate each and every one of you and your personal sacrifices for your country!

Respectfully, your fellow soldier,
Robert L. Scheck, U.S. Army

www.ingramcontent.com/pod-product-compliance
Lightning Source LLC
LaVergne TN
LVHW011941070526
838202LV00054B/4741